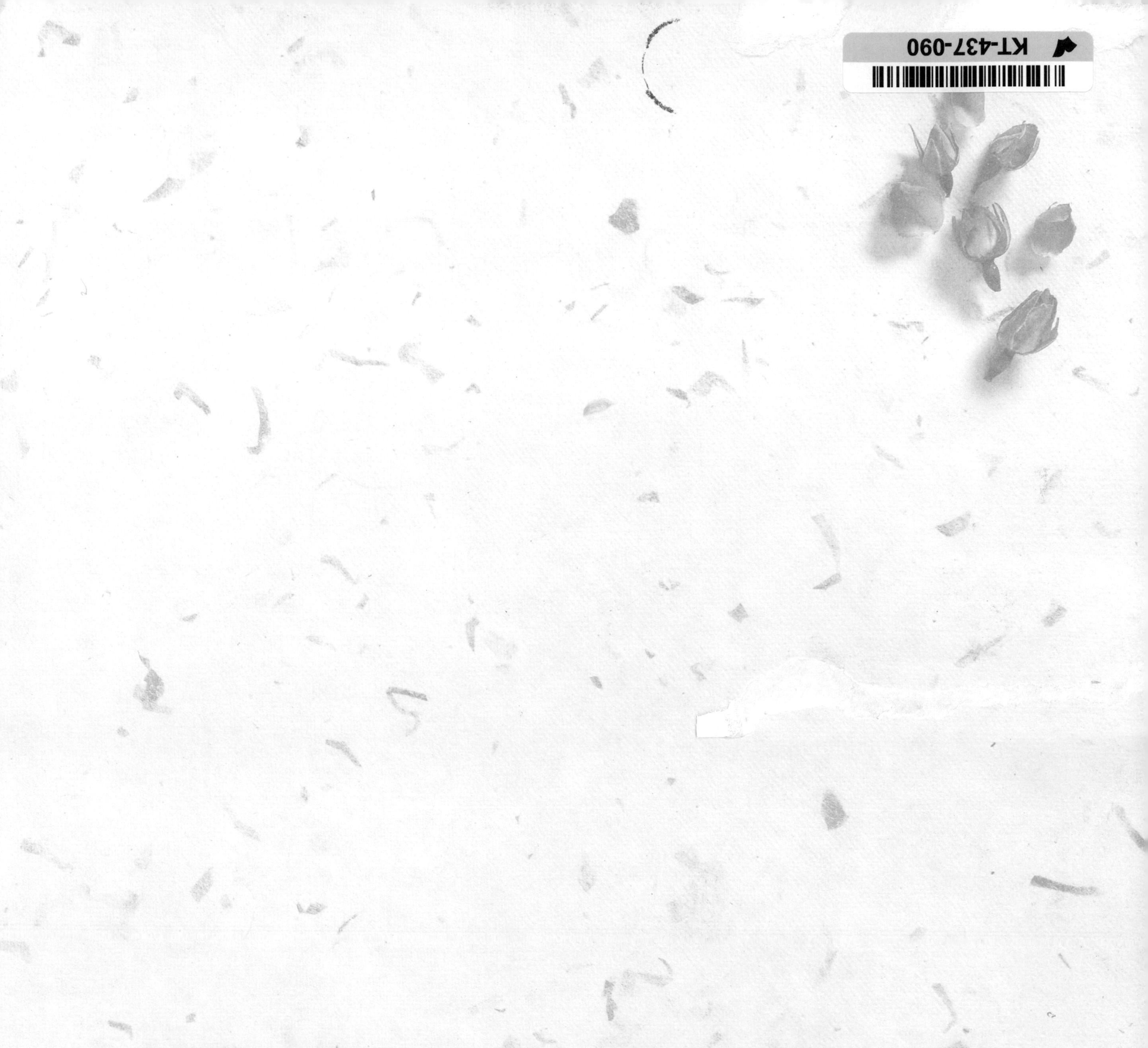

Making Memories

Making Memories

Scrapbook ideas for your treasured photographs and keepsakes

PENNY BOYLAN

LORENZ BOOKS

In loving memory of my father
Thomas Spence Jenkinson.

His photographs feature in many of the projects in this book, a poignant reminder of happy days spent with the family. He was always totally dependable and utterly devoted to all of us.

This edition published in 2000 by
Lorenz Books

Lorenz Books is an imprint of
Anness Publishing Limited
Hermes House
88–89 Blackfriars Road
London SE1 8HA

This edition is distributed in the USA by Lorenz Books,
Anness Publishing Inc., 27 West 20th Street,
New York, NY10011, (800) 354-9657

A CIP catalogue information for this book is available from
the British Library

Publisher: Joanna Lorenz
Project Editor: Simona Hill
Photographer: Nicki Dowey
Designer: Bobbie Colgate-Stone
Illustrators: Lucinda Ganderton
Editorial reader: Diane Ashmore
Production: Joanna King

Printed and bound in Hong Kong/China

1 2 3 4 5 6 7 8 9 10

Contents

Introduction

It has never been easier or cheaper to take good photographs. With the availability of user-friendly cameras and the wonders of new technology, even amateur photographers can take reasonably good pictures following a few basic guidelines. But if you have amassed a vast collection of photographs over the years, documenting every imaginable occasion, the problem is always what to do with them all. Photo albums are the obvious answer, but a far more interesting solution is to make a scrapbook (or several). Photos can then be stored together with mementoes to produce a unique collage of an occasion, and the resulting pages will have much more impact and meaning than pages and pages of pictures. The ideas in this book will inspire you to start making your own albums and album pages, and to organize and archive your treasured memories in attractive and creative ways.

Making the projects in this book has been great fun and highly rewarding. But you do not have to copy these projects slavishly.

Above: A romantic trip to Paris inspired this box covered in a colour photocopy of an old city plan of Paris.

Above: Old faded letters add a sense of history to a collage of old sepia photographs.

One of the main principles to follow when designing your pages is to let the photographs guide you in your choice of colours and textures. Photos often have their own particular colour as, for example, in the faded browns of old sepia photographs, but modern pictures have their own look too: see how well the strong reds and pinks of the babies work with the bright flower cut-outs.

Before you begin working on making albums and pages, sort through all your pictures carefully and organize them into clearly labelled sets. Handle photographs with care; the oils in your fingertips can damage the print. Write relevant details on the back of the print with a photo labelling pencil or soft pencil. Do not use permanent markers or ballpoint pens as these damage the paper. Store photographs carefully to preserve their condition. Sunlight obviously causes pictures, particularly colour prints, to fade, but the chemicals used to make some cardboards and papers can also cause deterioration. Choose good quality boxes and keep the pictures in sets in archival envelopes made from acid-free papers or in glassine envelopes especially made for photography. The plastics in some ready-made photo albums can also lead to damage from the chemicals used; the plastics become brittle with age, and may yellow and stick to the photographs. Look for plastics considered safe for direct contact with photographs, such as polypropylene, polythene and mylar. These are the best materials in which to store negatives safely. Film processing is reasonably inexpensive, so always try to have a duplicate set of prints made, especially for very important occasions. Black and white prints last longer than colour, so for really special occasions it may be a good idea to take a roll of black and white film to ensure the longevity of your archives. Another reason to have duplicates made is to give you the opportunity to have fun cutting and cropping prints.

The ultimate archivist can store photographs on CD-ROM; this service is offered at the same time as films are processed. One disk will hold hundreds of photographs with a minimum of storage space compared to boxes of prints. There is also computer software available for documenting your family tree and incorporating scanned photographs. They can be retrieved and prints made from the CD-ROM method as well.

Once you have sorted out your photographs and planned groups for different album pages, the fun begins. Scrapbooking is easy. All the projects have step-by-step instructions to guide you through the process. No great artistic skills are required, just patience, care and a little time. There is a huge range of materials and equipment on the market especially aimed at the scrapbook and album-making enthusiast. For best results use acid-free papers and adhesives. These are free from the chemicals that cause fading and yellowing when in contact with the photographs. Alternatively, using duplicates or colour photocopies is an ideal way around this problem. In this book we have tried not to rely on too many ready-made products for the projects. Most of the equipment consists of craft knives, scissors, rulers and glues; the materials and equipment section will guide you around everything we have used.

Above: Make copies of your favourite photographs for scrapbook collages, rather than use the originals.

Above: Natural foliage and pressed flowers are an obvious choice to decorate an album for an enthusiastic gardener.

In this fast-moving age when everything is "high tech", life moves at such a pace that we often miss out on the moment. Album-making is a way to keep in touch with our past, to keep our treasured photographs and memorabilia accessible to look through and enjoy from time to time. It is also a way of putting together memories for our future generations to enjoy. Have fun!

Techniques

Before you launch headlong into making album pages, there are a few basic techniques to master, ranging from tinting photographs and making backgrounds to framing pictures. These techniques will help you create an imaginative scrapbook and give your finished pages a more attractive look.

Equipment

Most people will find they already have the basic equipment that they need around the home, such as glue, a ruler, pencils, sharp scissors and a selection of photographs.

1 AIRBRUSH PEN
A fun way to give a lightly airbrushed effect.

2 ALBUM POSTS
Brass posts are used to hold album pages between their covers. They are available in varying lengths.

3 BULLDOG CLIPS
Use these to hold album pages together while you punch the holes.

4 BRUSHES
You will need a selection of artist's paint-brushes, a small household brush for spreading PVA (white) glue and a stencil brush for decorating papers with stencilled designs.

5 CORK MAT
This protects the work surface when doing pinpricking.

6 CRAFT KNIFE
Indispensable for trimming paper and cutting through thick cardboard.

7 CRAFT PUNCH
Use this to cut shapes from paper to leave a decorative hole. Use the punched motif as part of a collage design.

8 CUTTING MAT
A self-healing cutting mat protects the blade of your craft knife and the work surface.

9 EYELETS AND PUNCH (not shown)
Useful decorative devices for securing card (cardboard) in place. These can be bought from craft stores.

10 FABRIC ADHESIVE
Made specially for the purpose, allow to dry slightly before sticking fabrics together.

11 FABRIC TAPE
Use this adhesive tape when constructing the hinged part of an album cover.

12 GLUE STICK
This glue is clean and easy to use.

13 HAMMER
Used for tapping down on a wad punch (awl) when punching through layers of paper.

14 MASKING TAPE
Use for temporarily holding papers in place.

15 NICKEL RINGS
Available from stationery suppliers, these are used to make your own simple ring binders.

16 PENS AND PENCILS
You will need a soft pencil and a black pen in your basic kit.

17 PHOTO CORNERS
Use photo corners to hold your pictures in place. Choose from transparent self-adhesive corners, the gummed craft paper type, or black and gold versions.

18 PHOTO TINTING PAINTS
Use tinting paints to add touches of colour to black and white prints.

19 PVA (WHITE) GLUE
Available from DIY suppliers, this adhesive is cleaned from brush and roller with water.

20 REVOLVING LEATHER PUNCH
This tool makes several different sized holes in paper.

21 RUBBER STAMPS AND INK PADS
Available in a huge array of designs and colours for decorating backgrounds.

22 SCISSORS
You will need a good pair of paper scissors and a pair of fine decoupage scissors can be useful for delicate work. An excellent quick way to create mounts for your pictures is to use decorative-edge scissors. They are available in a huge range of designs.

23 SPONGE, ROLLER AND BRUSH
Use to apply paint or glue over large areas.

24 SPRAY ADHESIVE
This is useful for larger areas.

25 STENCIL CRAYONS (PAINTS)
Used dry, these oil-based crayons are easy to use. Make sure the work has dried out before adding photos; and protect the pages with a layer of glassine paper to prevent the colour transferring to other pages.

26 STENCILS
Use stencils to decorate backgrounds.

27 THREADS
You will need threads in various colours for all the sewing projects.

28 WAD PUNCH
A special tool for leathercraft; can be used to make clean holes through layers of paper.

23
19
12
10
24
21
18
27
21
20
7
21
2
13
6
3
22
P51
22
22
8
17
5
26
4
6
25
9
1
14
15
16
28
16
11
22

Materials

By far the most important materials you will need are a selection of decorative papers. If you wish the work to last in archival condition, use acid-free papers and adhesives. However, for most purposes, the wonderful choice of papers available will suffice. Colour, texture and weight are all a matter of personal choice, but here are a few guidelines to help you.

1 BRAIDS AND RIBBONS
Use these to frame your photographs.

2 CORRUGATED CARDBOARD
This is a good choice for making frames and mounts for pictures that deserve individual attention. Use it for photographs that will be on permanent display – it may squash between the heavy leaves of an album.

3 DECOUPAGE SCRAPS
Copies of the original Victorian scraps used for decoupage are available in packs from stationers. They are printed with a wide range of subjects and you will almost certainly find something suitable to match the theme of your work.

4 FABRIC
Use cotton or silk if you intend to transfer your photographs on to fabric. Natural fabrics are best for patchwork, since they wash and press easily, will not fray and do not distort while they are stitched together. Fabric can be stored in acid-free tissue paper to prolong its life.

5 GLASSINE PAPER
This is a special type of tissue that is waxy to the touch and transparent to look at. It is used for protecting photographs in albums and is interleaved between pages to protect the pictures from dust, and from colour or adhesives transferring between pages.

6 HEAVY CARDBOARD (not illustrated)
Use good quality cardboard for making album covers so that the boards will not buckle. Leave the covers under a weight to dry after covering with glues and papers. Dry thoroughly before assembling the album.

7 MEMORABILIA
This can include any items you hold dear: pebbles and shells collected from a beach, petals pressed from a posy of flowers, tickets for the theatre or a journey, an invitation to an event, certificates and ribbons of achievement, letters and foreign stamps, the list is almost endless.

8 PAPERS – HANDMADE
As the texture of some handmade papers can be uneven, ensure that they do not cause the photographs to buckle and bend by inter-leaving the pages or adding a divider page between heavily textured or embossed paper. Aim to use a wide range of colours and tex-tures in your work and choose papers that are sympathetic to the colours in the images.

9 PHOTOGRAPHS
You don't need a huge quantity of photographs to start making album pages, but until you are confident that you will get the effect you want, have copies of your pictures made before you start and work with a copy. Assemble the images into logical groups then choose your favourites for your pages.

10 STICKERS
For an almost instant effect, use stickers to decorate album pages. They are available in a huge selection of colours and styles.

11 WALLPAPER
This heavy-weight decorative paper can be a fun addition to your album pages – use its colour, pattern and texture as a background for your images. Doll's house wallpaper is also a good choice for small-scale designs.

12 WATERCOLOUR PAPER
This comes in many different qualities and is particularly attractive for making wedding album pages. The heavy paper is ideal for sticking photographs to since it won't buckle easily under the weight of the photographs. This type of paper is ideal to decorate with paint effects.

13 WRAPPING PAPER
There is a beautiful array of decorative papers available with specially designed and printed images celebrating specific events. These can be successfully used for album page or memory box backgrounds. Better still, preserve some of the paper used to wrap a special gift for the purpose.

3
7
4
7
8
13
5
7
13
11
11
7
7
2
10
9
1
1
12

Improving Photographs

Even if you are a good photographer, there will always be some pictures that don't come out right, with too much background, people disappearing off the edge of the photo or, especially on photographs taken with a flash, people with red eyes. Rather than throwing these pictures away, there are ways of improving them which will enable you to display them in your album.

Cropping Pictures

If you have a photograph where the main focus is off to one side, and the rest of the photo is sea or sky, it is easy to crop off the unwanted part of the picture, since only a plain colour is vying for attention with the main subject. If the subject is set against a busy background, the background will still compete for attention, even when a large part of it is cropped away.

Rather than cutting off the unwanted part of the picture by eye and ending up with a lopsided picture, use two pieces of black L-shaped card (card stock) which you can use to form a frame around the part of the picture you want to use. Adjust the L-shapes to the desired picture, then mark the photo with a pencil. Cut it out using a craft knife and metal ruler and working on a cutting mat. Cropping pictures will give you a variety of different-sized photographs, ensuring greater interest on the album page.

Above: Aim to centre the subject in the photo.

Left: These L-shaped cards frame the image, showing where the excess photograph can be cropped away.

Above: We all have images like this in our photo collection. Simply crop away all the sky to focus on the main subject.

Removing Red Eyes

This simple trick will improve all your photos of people with red eyes in an instant. Simply take a red eye pen (available in all good photograhic suppliers) and colour in all the red eyes visible on the photograph, taking care not to mark the rest of the faces. This pen is permanent so the colour will not smudge, and your pictures will look much better as a result.

Left: Red eyes appear when the subject is looking directly at the camera when the flash goes off. The problem is now easy to rectify with a red eye pen. Use it like a felt tip pen to colour out the unwanted red tones.

Tinting Photographs

Many black and white photographs, particularly those that have not had chance to age, can often look stark in a photograph album. One way to enliven them and give them more interest is to tint them with inks.

These inks are specially formulated for colouring photographs and are available in a range of colours. The most common use for these inks is in tinting flesh on black and white images. When doing this, however, take care not to overdo the inking, or the pictures will end up looking comic.

In a palette, add a drop of colour to some cold water solution. Water the colour sufficiently, paint it on the image, then add more colour if it is too weak. If you add too much colour to start with it cannot be removed easily. Test all the colours first on a copy of your photograph to ensure that you are happy with the effect and so that you do not ruin the originals.

1 Select the photographs to be inked. Pour some water mixed with solution in a shallow tray. Using a pair of tweezers, add one photo at a time to the solution.

2 Place the wet photo on a board and wipe the excess water from it using a cloth. The photo should be damp rather than wet, or the ink will run where the water is rather than where you want it to go. Prepare some inks with solution.

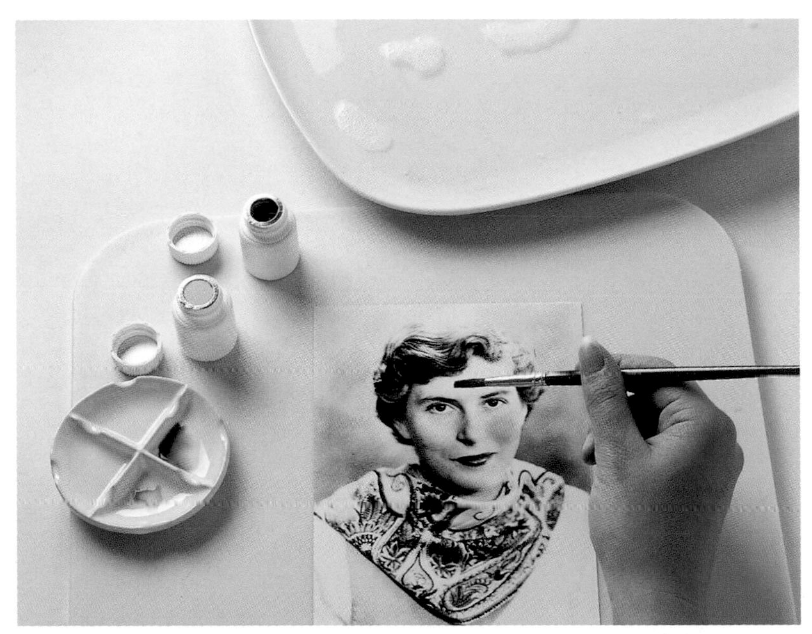

3 Begin by adding colour to the face using a fine paintbrush. Apply the colour gently and wait for it to be dispersed by the damp print before adding more colour. Test the colours first to see how different the dry colour appears to the wet colour.

4 Add touches of colour to the hair, eyes and lips. Darken the colour as necessary to suit the person in the photograph. Finally, add touches of colour to the clothing. Leave the photo to dry thoroughly between colours.

Background Treatments

Rather than have blank backgrounds to the pages in your photo album, decorate them with stamps, stencils, stickers and paint effects in colours and themes that are sympathetic to your photographs. Choose subdued, muted shades for subtle compositions, or be more adventurous and experiment with unusual combinations of colour. The treatments mentioned here are all suitable for everyone to tackle.

Choosing Backgrounds

Allow the photographs to dictate the choice of background colours to use, rather than choosing a background and hoping the photographs will fit. Hold your images against a wide variety of papers with patterns, colours and textures before making a final decision.

The background should be sympathetic to your photographs rather than overpower them and should enhance the subject matter. Rather than using just one paper for the background, make up a collage of interesting textures and patterns. Include greetings cards, wrapping paper, children's artwork, and even fabric swatches.

Above: Do not shy away entirely from patterned backgrounds; these scraps of wallpaper work beautifully with the warm tones of the cat.

Left: If you place the same images on a different background with colours that clash with the photographs, you can instantly see that it is is an unsuitable combination.

Decorative Paint Effects

Mix some acrylic paint together with wallpaper paste to make a thick paste. Using a large paintbrush, paint the surface of a sheet of heavy cartridge (white) paper using even strokes in one direction.

Before the paint mixture dries, make patterns in the paint using a variety of objects such as the blunt end of a paintbrush, a cocktail stick (toothpick) or wooden skewer. Cut a comb from a piece of cardboard and move it in a wavy line through the paint to create a variety of different effects.

Allow the paper to dry completely. Do not worry if it is buckled; simply iron the back with a cool domestic iron and press it between heavy books to keep flat.

Above: The effect above was obtained by cutting a regular pattern into a piece of thick cardboard. Experiment with different patterns.

Above: Just a few of the effects that can be achieved by scraping paint away. Try using a fork, wire, cotton buds, or empty felt-tipped pens.

Rubber Stamping

1 There are literally hundreds of rubber stamps available on the market nowadays, so you will always be able to find something to complement your album page designs. Use a single motif to stamp an all-over design on to plain paper to create a patterned background. Press the stamp in the ink pad, then press it on the paper, taking care not to smudge. Repeat as desired.

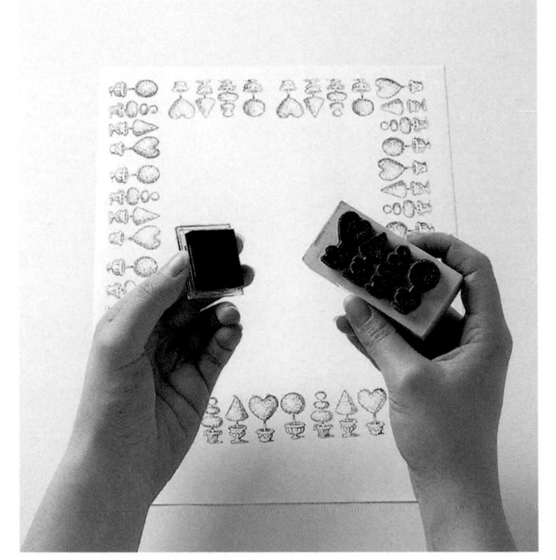

2 The elongated shape of this topiary stamp makes it ideal for a border design. If you want the design to fit the page precisely, you can measure the stamp and work out how many repeats will fit the page. To stamp a border design, ensure the stamp aligns with the page, and that each new print lines up with the design already stamped.

3 Rubber-stamped designs can be enhanced very simply by colouring them in lightly with coloured pencils. You could also try using various kinds of paint to achieve different effects.

Antiquing with Tea

Many of the projects in this book have a background of aged or old-fashioned paper, either covered with text or with pictures. To achieve this antiqued effect, photocopy the text or picture in black and white, then gently brush a strong solution of tea over the whole surface. Tea, however, is acidic, so if you wish to take extra care of a precious photograph, substitute good quality writing or watercolour ink diluted to a suitable strength in place of the tea.

Allow the paper to dry, then press with a cool iron if necessary to flatten. The paper can then be torn or cut up to use as part of a collage. You could also try burning the edges of letters if they are to be used for the background collage for an interesting effect.

Above: A strong solution of cold tea will age paper or fabric instantly. Deckle the edges of the paper to add to the antique effect.

Using an Airbrush Pen

To create a spray-painted background, draw a heart shape on a piece of paper and cut it out. Position the shape on the background. Using an airbrush, spray paint evenly around the heart. Lift the shape away carefully and reposition as necessary. You can also use the heart template itself as part of the design.

Stencilling

1 Trace your design, then transfer the image on to oiled stencil card with a pencil. Go over the outlines with a black marker if necessary. Carefully cut out the stencil with a sharp craft knife. Work on a self-healing cutting mat or board to protect the work surface.

2 Rub a patch of stencil crayon (paint) in a circular motion on a spare area of the stencil. Load the stencil brush with colour from this until the brush is well coated. Brush the colour on to the paper using small circular movements to work the colour into small areas. Allow to dry.

3 Cut out a second stencil showing just the markings of the giraffe. Line up the giraffe's spots with the stencilled body and apply the colour as before. Add a tail and eyes with stencil crayon. Clean the brush with spirit. Stencil crayon is oil based and should be left for several days to dry out thoroughly.

TRANSFERRING PHOTOGRAPHS ON TO FABRIC

Several types of special paper are available for transferring photographs on to fabric. Your pictures will not be damaged by the process but it must be undertaken at a photocopy bureau. Copy several photographs together on to one sheet. Make sure you have enough transfers made to allow for experimentation and the odd mishap. Some photographs do not work well on the transfer paper, such as those with dark backgrounds or lots of contrast, so be prepared for some trial and error.

1 Stick the photographs lightly on to a piece of plain paper. Take this to a colour copy bureau together with the sheets of transfer paper. The transfer paper will have to be fed one sheet at a time through the paper tray. Have the photographs copied on a normal colour process to check that the colour is correct before proceeding to copy them on to the transfer paper.

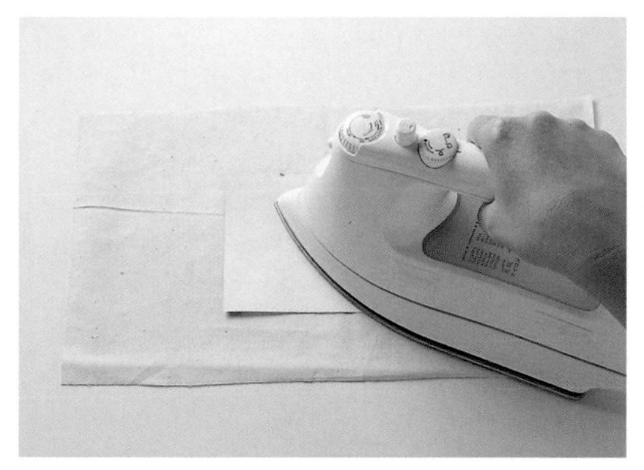

2 Trim around the transfers and place each one face down on to your chosen fabric. It is best to use plain natural fabric with a close weave, such as calico, as it will have to withstand heat and pressure. Always refer to the manufacturer's instructions. Press the backing of the transfer paper with an iron. If a great deal of pressure is required, work on a firm surface such as a kitchen table protected with several layers of blanket.

3 Carefully peel off the transfer backing in an even movement to reveal the transferred image. Allow the fabric to cool before using it. Directions for washing and aftercare should be on the instructions with the transfer paper. A more expensive, but generally foolproof method of photo transfer is to have the process done professionally at a copy bureau that prints T-shirts with your own images.

Left: Old black and white family photographs make interesting subjects for photographic transfer. Once the image has been transferred you could tea-dye the fabric for a faded antique look, in keeping with the style of the photographs.

HISTORICAL NOTE

Old American patchwork quilts, known as album quilts, often featured photographs (rather than transfers) as well as other items of ephemera in the quilt design. The blocks of the quilt designs were often made by different family members, and through images told the life story of the recipient. Such quilts provide a valuable personal, historical and political record of the times in which they were made, when written records would perhaps not have been made and kept by the family.

Framing and Mounting Pictures

There are a variety of ways to frame your favourite photographs or cards. They are all quick to do and very effective. Use a different idea for each occasion.

Making Cut-out Shapes

You can use pre-printed stickers for decorating many pages, but it is easy to make your own. Look for motifs in books and magazines as a guide, and trace or copy them on to plain paper. If you want to adjust the scale, this is easily done on a photocopier. Draw around the template or trace the design on to coloured paper and cut out carefully. Cut out any details with a craft knife, working on a cutting mat to protect the working surface.

Stick the shapes on to your album page, taking care not to allow glue to seep under the edges. Always smooth over glued images with a spare piece of paper; baking parchment is excellent for this.

Above and right: Children will enjoy making and decorating fun album pages with these simple cut-out designs.

Cropping Images

1 Using an oval-shaped stencil, mark out the shape for cropping a photo. Place the stencil over the area of the photo you have selected and gently draw through the shape with a very sharp, hard pencil.

2 Cut out the pencilled shape with fine-pointed scissors. You can then use the cut-out photo in an oval picture frame, or add it to a collage of different-shaped photos.

Making an Oval Mount

Using an oval stencil, make an aperture in some watercolour paper. Place the paper on a cork mat or similar soft surface. Using a darning needle, with gentle pressure pierce a design through the paper around the aperture. Wrap the needle in some masking tape to make it easier to hold. Experiment with different gauge needles.

Using Decorative Scissors

Another idea for a simple pinpricked mount is to cut around a rectangular piece of paper with deckle-edged scissors, then follow the wavy lines with a pinpricked outline. Decorative edges are easily achieved in this way. These are great fun to use and very good for an instant effect.

Using Stickers

These photographs were mounted on a strong blue background, then edged with butterfly stickers.

Corner Edgers

You can buy punches that will decorate corners as well as punch out motifs. Special scissors are available and are very easy to use. Line the paper up with the arrow on the scissors and cut in a single motion. Turn the scissors over to make a curved corner. Experiment with different-coloured, layered mounts for your photographs.

Using a Decorative Punch

There are lots of designs of punches available to choose from, including swirls, cherubs, hearts and teddy bears. You can make confetti to slip into memorabilia envelopes using punch-out motifs, or stick them on the envelope as decoration. Try punching a motif in just the corners of a mount, or in rows along the edges of a photo mailer or photo background mount.

Framing a Wedding Image

Cut a heart shape in gold paper slightly larger than the cropped photograph. Make slits in the heart template at each of the four corners of the photograph using a craft knife. Slip the photo into the slits. Enlarge or reduce the heart for different-sized photographs, or simply mount the heart on to decorated paper or card to send as a mailer to family and friends.

Inspirational Ideas

The following projects will give you an insight into the huge range of ideas you can follow in scrapbooking. Be inspired by the colours, textures and themes and try to adapt the ideas with your own photographs. Once you start, you will undoubtedly come up with many more ideas of your own.

Traditional Schemes
Floral Inspiration
Black and White
With Children in the Frame
Bold and Colourful
Natural Inspiration
Pale and Pastel

Traditional Schemes

As well as collections of old photographs, most of us have a pile of ephemera we just can't bear to get rid of, such as old wedding invitations, school reports, travel and theatre tickets, and so on. Here are some ideas for customizing ready-made boxes, album covers and decorative pages.

◄ These exquisite squares of Japanese origami paper, beautifully printed in stunning colours, were too good to cut up. Instead, they were used to form a framework for slightly faded sepia family portraits in a simple page layout.

A sturdy narrow box with an angled lid was the perfect shape for keeping thank-you letters and guest lists, as well as old receipts for wedding flowers and other items from the big day. The box was sprayed all over with several coats of ivory pearlized spray paint and allowed to dry. The cake motif was cut from the same ivory card used for the invitations and decorated with relief outliner in a pearlized white. This was then mounted on a tall heart shape cut from another piece of card in yet another shade of pearlized white. Keep the contents carefully wrapped in archival-safe glassine envelopes or other archival-safe covers away from the harmful effects of dust and light. ►

◄ This small box originally contained jewellery, but is the perfect shape and size for keeping mementoes of a beloved pet, such as the name tag and pedigree certificate. The photograph was transferred on to fabric, then stuck to the lid over a piece of wadding to pad it gently. The raw edges were covered with ribbon, then finished with the tops of decorative paper fasteners (you could also use buttons). The bottom of the box was painted gold to match the ribbon and complement the colours in the photo.

This Scottie dog album can be made and decorated in the same way as the Wedding Album project. Wrap the front and back jacket in suitable tartan paper, add corrugated cardboard over the spine and bind the pages together with ribbon instead of album posts. Small motifs of Scottie dogs, made from felt, decorate the front of the album, and a name plate has been pinned in place. ►

Floral Inspiration

Flowers and foliage can be used in so many different ways to decorate treasure boxes or embellish album covers and pages. Press petals from your favourite flowers, or collect leaf skeletons – even artificial flowers can be used to great effect.

The textures and subtle colours of handmade papers are irresistible to most people. This simple album is tied with handmade string through holes punched with a leather tool. The collage is made from a collection of stamped motifs, old postage stamps and pressed leaves with the addition of further textured papers and tissues all torn to shape. Brush any pressed leaves you use with a thin coat of PVA (white) glue to help preserve them.

A large spiral-bound sketchbook covered in a plain manila board was jazzed up into a fun photo album with the addition of artificial flowers. First a square of dyed hessian (available from craft shops) was glued in place. Irregular rectangles of handmade Japanese papers were then arranged in a grid format on the hessian, then the tops of artificial yellow flowers were snipped off their stems and glued down with strong wood adhesive. Choose different sizes and shapes of flowers keeping to a single colour theme, or go mad and use a whole jumble of bright funky colours on a piece of green artificial grass available from dolls' house suppliers.

◀ This box is a suitable shape for storing bulkier items. It was designed to keep on display in any interior setting, hence the neutral shades of natural decoration. The box was covered with handmade plant paper, then a very large dried leaf was glued on top and smaller ones around the sides of the box. Finally, scraps of shot organdie in similar colouring were arranged on top of the leaf on the lid.

▲ The faded browns of these old sepia photographs suggested a background of faded handwriting. This was achieved by photocopying old letters and documents, then staining them with tea or diluted inks. The papers were then torn and glued down, and the photographs were added using gummed brown photo corners. As a finishing touch, pressed leaves were carefully stuck down with a little PVA (white) glue. Protect the page in your album with a covering sheet of lens tissue or glassine paper.

Black and White

Black and white designs set a bold and classic tone, and make old black and white photographs look thoroughly contemporary. Textured papers and bright splashes of colour stop the images fading into the background.

◀ Layers of fine white corrugated card (card stock) make up an ornate frame for a wedding picture. The oval aperture was cut out using a stencil. Remember that pressure on the ridges will flatten them, so work with a new blade in your scalpel to cut out the shape. The paper was folded in half to get a symmetrical design.

The sophisticated larger album is made in the same way as the Wedding Album project, but tied with black grosgrain ribbon instead of album posts. Its smaller partner was a ready-made spiral-bound album with an aperture cut in the cover. This was edged with a piece of the same black glossy crocodile embossed paper. The corners were trimmed and glued to cover the edges of the aperture, then a thin square of pink foil paper was stuck on the inside cover to close the aperture. ▶

The cover for this landscape album is made of photocopies. Both colour and black and white photographs were photocopied on a colour printer in black and white to give a better texture and finish. The pictures were trimmed and arranged in a collage on black paper. This was laminated and spiral-bound with more blank black pages tucked inside to form a photo album. Remember to include a laminated back page as well.

This album page is designed for storing extra prints or paper memorabilia in an attractive functional way. Printed *toile de jouy* fabric was photocopied on a colour laser printer. The copies were mounted on to black paper using spray adhesive. An envelope was cut out from the photocopied paper (see Templates), then the flaps were folded down with a bone folder, and slits added with a scalpel to thread with ribbon. The side pocket was trimmed with fancy-edged scissors and a strip of the same ribbon was added to balance the design. The components were glued together and mounted on a larger piece of card (card stock) chosen to complement the ribbon.

With Children in the Frame

Children's pictures suggest bright and colourful frames, backgrounds and mounts – try using a piece of artwork for a background or greetings cards for decoration.

▲ This album was made from an iridescent ring binder. Brightly coloured decoupage scraps were glued on to irregular rectangles of pearlized papers and arranged in a design on the front cover.

This fun album cover features copies of children's faces cut out and stuck on to flower pictures. Two holes have been punched through the folded cover and the album pages, and a bunch of raffia threaded through and tied in a bow. ▲

Keep special handmade cards and use them together with photographs to make a lovely memento. Mount them on a coloured background, then glue the background to a piece of paper in a contrasting colour to make a frame. ►

◄ Every parent collects their offspring's artwork, only for it to be put aside to curl and gather dust. This solution uses colour-copied children's drawings and paintings, together with early pieces of writing and other handmade artwork as a background for photographs.

Bold and Colourful

Bright colours add a cheerful tone to any display of photographs or memorabilia and are sure to make a conversation point. This quirky wreath brings together all those photographs you've been wondering how to display in a bold and attractive way.

◂ A picture wreath is a good way to display a lot of pictures together. Unwanted backgrounds were trimmed off photographs to focus on people's faces, then the photos were arranged in layers around a circle of flexible board. This wreath was assembled from three different sizes of circle; the smallest one using the smaller cut-outs. The circles were then stuck together in layers for a slightly three-dimensional effect.

◂ A selection of brightly-coloured blank greetings cards with apertures have been bound together with metal rings. A photograph has been mounted on each card. The cover is cut from translucent polythene to create a compact album.

▴ This is more of a folder than an album. It contains single pages for adding photos or documents. The handmade cover was bought ready punched with a fretwork design. Simply folded into three and tied with a bright ribbon, this is an easily-made keepsake album.

◂ This album page uses contemporary motifs to good effect as a change from the more sentimental designs usually associated with baby pictures. Silver card-board makes a suitable background for holographic stickers. The daisy motifs have been cut from complementary-coloured plain paper.

Natural Inspiration

Let the muted shades of nature inspire your collage designs. Gathered natural objects such as twigs, pebbles and shells are intrinsic to all these designs which present unusual methods for storing treasured collections of ephemera.

A ready-made artist's portfolio like this one can be decorated simply by covering the foundation with your choice of textured paper, then adding a favourite print to the front.

▲ This seaside display was made by filling a purchased box frame with a layer of shells, gathered over a series of seaside holidays. A simple background was made with tinted paper and a strip of sky torn from a magazine. A special photograph was added for a lovely open display. If you like, you could make two or three similar box frames and arrange them together to create a seaside series.

Dried twigs *(above left)* have been glued to corrugated cardboard and backed with a heavy cardboard frame to make this novel log book.

◀ This delightful album cover has been covered in painted textured paper and simply decorated with a scallop. The inside pages are filled in the same way as the Contemporary Collection project.

Pale and Pastel

Pale and pastel colours suit cute and cuddly images of young babies and complement the faded tones of old sepia photographs.

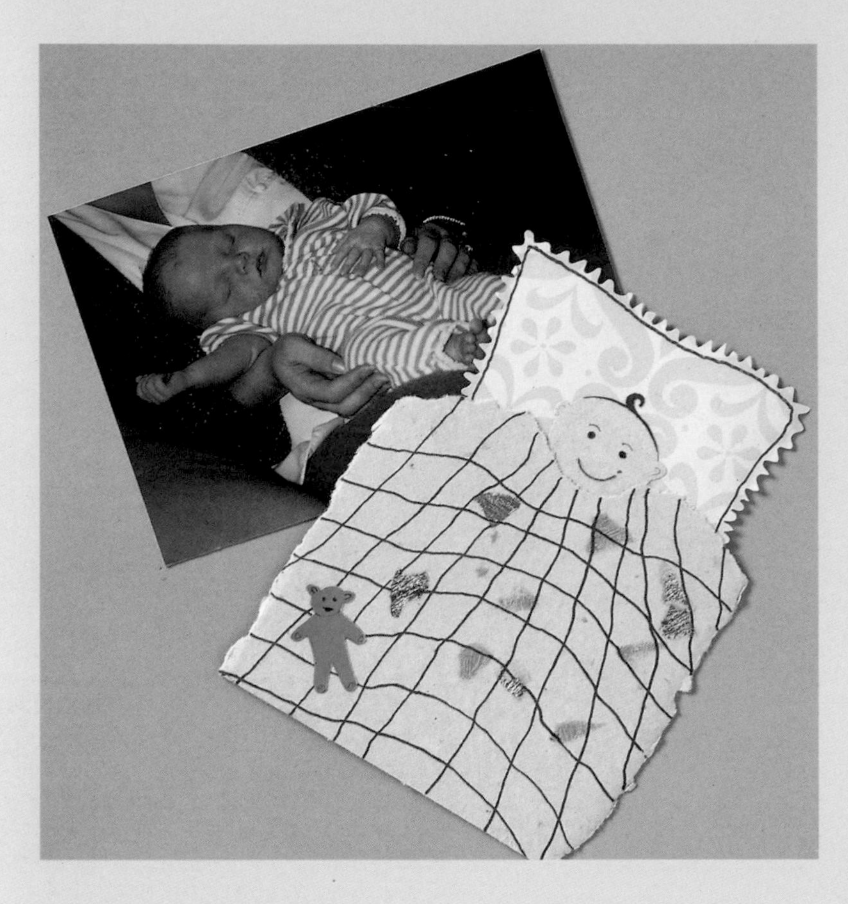

A cute handmade birthday card and a pretty background colour were all that was needed to make an attractive album page from a single photograph.

Purchased ring binders are perfect for making customized album covers. Here, a piece of felt was cut to fit the front and back of the binder with extra deep flaps folded inside. The purchased motif was glued with fabric adhesive to a patch of felt and stitched in place on the front cover. The binder was lightly glued to the felt to hold it in place and the edges were blanket-stitched all around.

◀ As a change from the more usual forms of birth announcement, why not make these simple origami envelopes to send out to family and friends? Use plain or printed paper and slot ribbon through small punched holes to decorate the front. You can add a little label with the birth details written on it too. Slip a colour photocopy or an original print, if you have made plenty of duplicates, inside the envelope. Add a copy of the baby's footprint for a grandparent to keep and write your message on the reverse.

The creamy pages in this ready-made album are decorated with decoupaged photocopies of old botanical illustrations. The images were lightly tinted by colouring in with crayons, before being cut out with sharp pointed scissors. Treasured squares of costly origami paper in a crinkly texture were used as backgrounds for the flowers, which were carefully glued down. The photographs were attached with transparent photo corners. ▶

The Projects

These projects record a range of different occasions as album pages, covers, treasure boxes and free-standing displays. Step-by-step instructions allow you to follow these ideas closely, or you can choose to use them as a springboard for your own pages, inspired by your own particular photographs and mementoes.

Accordion Picture Album ❖ Seaside Memory Board
Album for a Baby Girl ❖ Wedding Album
Travel Memorabilia Album Pages
Decoupage Memory Box
Flowery Faces Album Pages ❖ Our House
Picnic in the Park ❖ Patchwork Album Covers
Album Page for a Baby Boy ❖ Pets' Page
Folk Art Album Pages ❖ Schooldays
Family Tree ❖ Wedding Page
Memory Quilt ❖ Christmas Scraps Page
Contemporary Collection ❖ Family in the Garden
Fabric-covered Memory Box ❖ Butterfly Bonanza

Accordion Picture Album

Make this pretty accordion album for all your favourite photographs. Choose a selection of luxurious decorative papers in similar shades of mauve for a really striking effect.

MATERIALS

Large rubber stamp in a leaf motif
Metallic stamping ink pad
Translucent paper
Craft knife
Thick cardboard
Metal ruler
Cutting mat
Decorative metallic paper
Bone folder
Glue stick
Handmade paper

1 Stamp the motif on to a selection of papers to choose the effect you like best. To do this, press the stamp into the ink pad to coat the surface with ink, then press the stamp on the paper. Lift it up carefully to avoid smudging. Here, the motif was stamped on translucent paper using metallic ink. Take care when stamping on to tracing paper, as some stamping inks do not dry well on the resistant surface. If you have difficulty, stamp on a lightweight handmade paper instead. Cut out the motif with a craft knife.

2 To make the front and back covers of the album, cut two pieces of thick cardboard to the required size using a craft knife and metal ruler, and working on a cutting mat. Then cut two pieces of decorative metallic paper 2.5cm (1in) larger all around than the cardboard. Glue one piece of cardboard to the centre of each piece of paper. Cut across the corners of the metallic paper, then glue the edges and carefully fold them over to stick them down securely on the cardboard. Turn the front cover over and glue the stamped leaf motif in the centre.

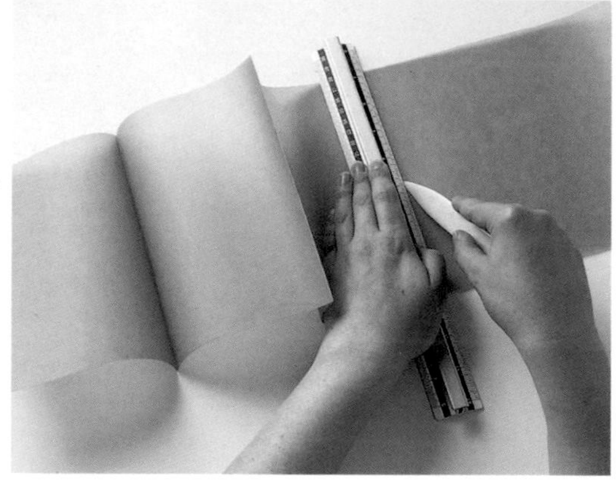

3 Cut a long strip of translucent paper slightly narrower than the height of the cover board. This will form the accordion centre of the album. Measure the width of the album cover and make folds along this strip of paper to match. To do this, carefully and accurately measure the distance from one fold to another; use a metal ruler and bone folder to crease and score the paper to produce a succession of accordion folds. When you have finished, ensure that the paper folds into a neat pile, and that it fits neatly inside the album.

4 Stick one end of the folded translucent paper on to the front cover of the album, then cover the whole with another sheet of handmade paper to co-ordinate with the rest of the album. Stick the other end of the translucent paper to the back cover and cover this with handmade paper as before. Place the book under a heavy weight to prevent it from buckling as it dries.

Seaside Memory Board

This collection of holiday memories serves both as a decorative display and as a noticeboard on which other mementoes can be added from time to time. It could even be used as a memo board for day-to-day reminders. Precious old photographs fade easily, so it is a good idea to have copies made of the pictures you are using to keep them safe.

MATERIALS

Seaside holiday (vacation) photographs
Magazine pictures of sea, sand, pebbles, shells, etc
Old maps with large areas of sea
Feathers, small shells, etc
Scissors
Metal ruler
Craft knife
Lightweight board or other non-flexible surface
Textured paper in complementary colours
Acid-free spray adhesive
Transparent photo corners

1 Spread out your collection of photographs, pictures, maps and seaside ephemera. Cut out some of the pictures with scissors, tear some to give them a ragged edge, and trim others with a metal ruler and craft knife so that you have a range of different textures and edges to the collection.

2 Assemble the larger pictures of sky and sea on the board, overlapping them with areas of textured paper to make a background for the photographs. When you are happy with the arrangement, glue the pictures down thoroughly with spray adhesive. Arrange a feather or piece of seaside ephemera on the board.

3 Complete the memory board by securing your photographs to the board using transparent photo corners; if you have duplicate photographs, you could stick them in position with glue. Using photo corners enables you to place other mementoes behind the photos as your collection grows.

— TIP —

To tear heavy-weight paper, fold the edge to be torn against a metal ruler. Crease the fold with your finger nail or a bone folder. Dampen the paper with a fine paintbrush and cold water, then tear it carefully. Allow the paper to dry before applying it to the project, and if necessary, iron it if it has buckled.

Album for a Baby Girl

This charming project provides an ideal way to display your favourite baby pictures and will become a family heirloom to be treasured. Make one for each new child in the family, or give them as presents to expectant parents or doting grandparents.

MATERIALS

Metal ruler
Craft knife
Cutting mat
Sheet of self-adhesive mount board
Pencil
Polyester wadding (batting), 35 x 33cm (14 x 13in)
Scissors
Two pieces of fabric, 35 x 33cm (14 x 13in)
Glue stick
Masking tape
Photograph, 15 x 10cm (6 x 4in)
Watercolour paper, 3 x 30cm (1¼ x 12in)
Stickers
Hole punch
20 sheets of watercolour paper, 29 x 27cm (11¾ x 10¾in)
Ribbon

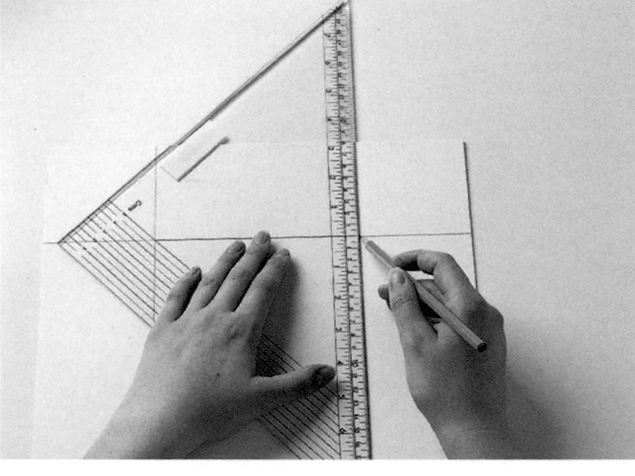

1 Using a metal ruler and craft knife and working on a cutting mat, cut out three rectangles each 30 x 28cm (12 x 11in) and one rectangle 30 x 25cm (12 x 10in) from the self-adhesive mount board. On the smaller rectangle, using a ruler or set square and pencil, draw a border 8cm (3¼in) all around from the outer edge. This will form the aperture for the photograph.

2 Using a craft knife, cut out the central rectangle and discard it; you will now have a rectangular frame. Peel off the protective paper from the mount board and stick a piece of wadding (batting) over the frame. Trim the wadding to the same size as the mount board with scissors.

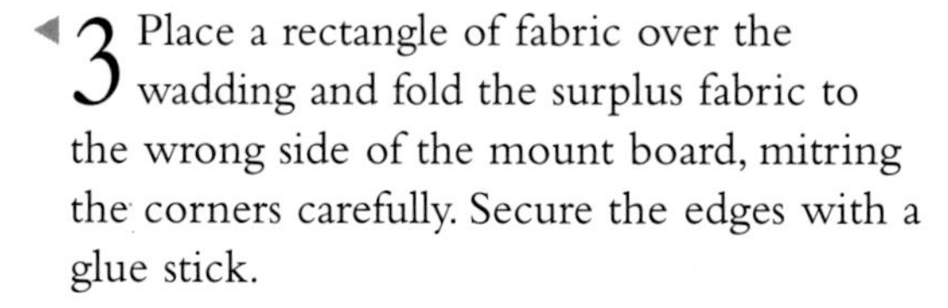

3 Place a rectangle of fabric over the wadding and fold the surplus fabric to the wrong side of the mount board, mitring the corners carefully. Secure the edges with a glue stick.

4 Cut two diagonal slits in the centre of the fabric and fold the surplus fabric triangles to the back. Secure with a glue stick. Tape the photograph face down over the centre of the back of the padded frame so that the picture is visible from the padded fabric side.

5 Peel the paper from one of the larger rectangles of mount board. Fix the narrow strip of watercolour paper on to one long edge, then stick the padded frame in place over the rest of the mount board so that the watercolour paper is on the left of the frame. Press down firmly to secure. Using a craft knife, score along the line where the paper and frame join, to enable the cover to open flat. Cover the second large mount board rectangle with fabric. Stick the third mount board rectangle to the wrong side of the fabric-covered board to form the back cover.

6 Position one coloured sticker at each corner of the photograph at the front of the album to disguise any raw edges. For extra security for the stickers, dab a tiny spot of glue from a glue stick on to the fabric as well.

7 Punch two holes in the centre of the left edge of the front and back covers and the sheets of watercolour paper; the paper will form the album pages. Position the front and back covers on each side of the pages and lace them together with ribbon.

8 Tie the ribbon ends in a bow. Add a few more stickers above and below the bow along the strip of watercolour paper to complete.

Wedding Album

This wedding album is made in traditional shades of cream, but it is unfussy and contemporary in its design. A beautiful handmade album makes a perfect gift for the bride and groom.

MATERIALS

Craft knife
Metal ruler
Cutting mat
Heavy duty cardboard
Lightweight cotton cloth
Fabric glue
Bone folder
Cream leather-look textured paper
Scissors
PVA (white) glue
Small roller and tray
Paintbrush
Cream grosgrain ribbon
Rosebud ribbon, or other wedding trimming
Pencil
Hammer
Wad punch (awl)
Cream paper for the album pages
Bulldog clips
Two brass album posts

1 Using a sturdy craft knife and metal ruler and working on a cutting mat, cut the board to the size you require for the album cover. For the hinged section, cut a strip 2.5cm (1in) wide off the heavy duty cardboard down one short side to make the hinge: it should be wide enough to take the album posts.

2 Cut a strip of lightweight cotton cloth to join the pieces of board together and glue it down on one side of the cardboard to make a flexible hinge. Press down firmly with a bone folder to secure. This side will be the inside of the album cover.

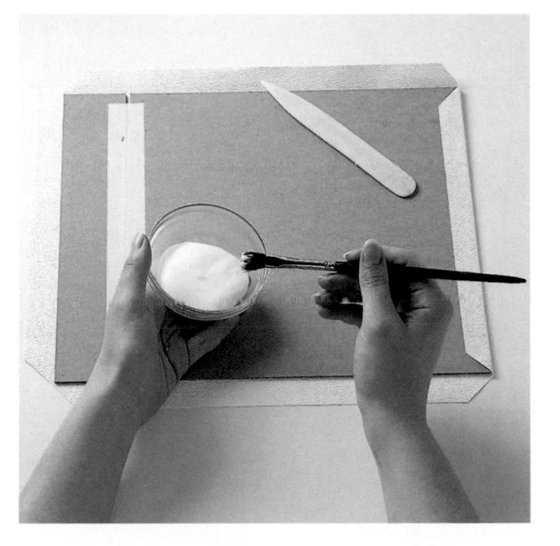

3 Cut a piece of leather-look paper slightly larger all around than the album cover. Apply PVA (white) glue to the paper using a small roller. Glue the cardboard to the paper. Working on the inside cover, trim the corners of the paper and brush glue on to the flaps, then stick them down to the cardboard, easing the corners and smoothing them down with the bone folder. Take care when smoothing embossed papers that you do not press too hard and eliminate the texture. Make a back cover in the same way. Keep both covers under heavy weights for a day or two until they are completely dry to prevent them from buckling.

4 Stick a length of cream grosgrain ribbon across the centre of the front cover using fabric glue sparingly. Allow the glue to dry slightly before sticking down the ribbon to help avoid excess glue seeping through the ribbon. When this is dry, glue a length of rosebud ribbon along the top of the grosgrain. Turn the album cover over and glue a piece of paper over the inside of the cover to hide the raw edges of the ribbon and the flaps of cover paper. Use the same paper as that used for the cover or a piece of matching heavyweight cream paper that will not show the bumps made by the ribbon. Glue down the endpapers.

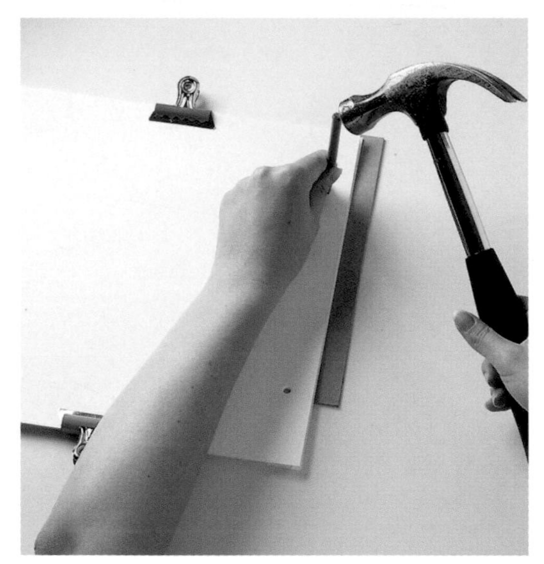

5 Mark the position for the album posts on the hinge of the album cover. Working on a spare piece of heavy cardboard to protect the surface, gently hammer the wad punch (awl) through each marked position to make a clean hole for the posts to be threaded through. Repeat for the back cover. Collate the album pages, and trim them to size so they are slightly smaller than the cover. Hold them together firmly in a batch with bulldog clips and make holes with the wad punch exactly matching those for the album posts.

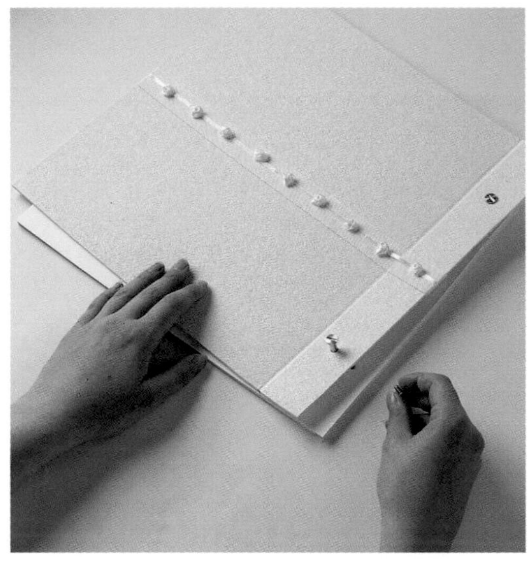

6 To assemble the album, thread the album posts through the front cover, the pages and the back cover. Tighten the screws to secure each in place.

Travel Memorabilia Album Pages

This collection of memorabilia from a vacation in Spain is attractively displayed in a practical way with functional pockets in which to slip airline tickets, restaurant bills, postcards and other bits and pieces picked up during the trip. A photo-montage of attractive places can be made from a duplicate set of pictures.

MATERIALS

Craft knife
Metal ruler
Cutting mat
Red card (card stock)
Masking tape
Marking pen or pencil
Bradawl (awl)
Small nickel eyelets and eyelet tool
Hammer
Pictures, photographs and memorabilia
Bone folder
Glue stick
Assorted paperclips

1 Using a craft knife and metal ruler and working on a cutting mat, cut out three background squares from red card (card stock). Put two squares aside. Cut out a smaller square from red card and tape this to the centre of one large square. Mark on the small square the positions for four eyelets, one in each corner. At each marked point make a small hole to fit the size of the eyelets using a bradawl (awl). Insert an eyelet through both squares at each hole and secure in position at the back with a gentle tap of a hammer. Tickets, pictures and other travel memorabilia can now be slipped underneath the edges of the small square.

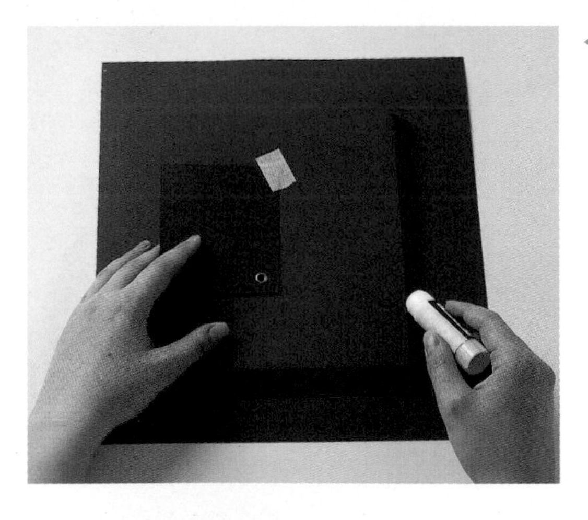

◀ 2 To make a page with a pocket, cut out a square of red card and attach a smaller piece of red card to it with an eyelet. Using a bone folder, score around two adjacent edges of the square to make flaps. Trim the corner and score again to make a neat crease. Glue the flaps to one of the large red background squares of card. Holiday memorabilia, such as tickets, stamps and notes can now be inserted in the flap pocket or attached to the pocket with paper clips.

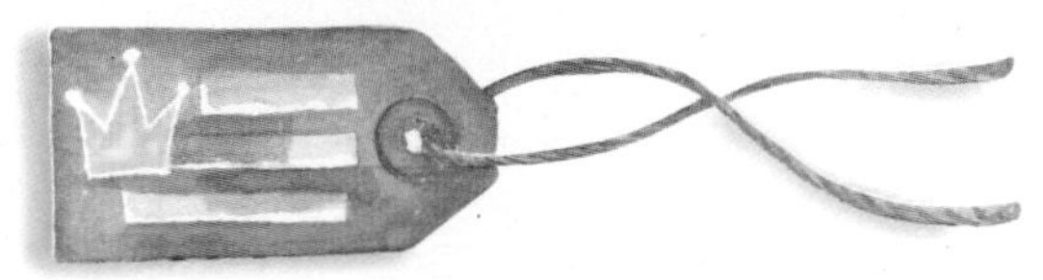

— TIP —

Photo montages look best when photographs have similar background colouring in them.

3 To create the photo-montage, arrange the pictures and photographs in a pleasing way on the last square of red card. Then trim away unnecessary parts of the photograph using a craft knife and a metal ruler, and working on a cutting mat. Using glue, stick the pictures in place.

futur
Àrea metropolitana de Barcelona
Entitat del transport
EL DISSENY A BARCELONA

Decoupage Memory Box

Decoupage is the art of decorating with cut-out scraps of paper. The pieces are overlaid and varnished to give the appearance of a hand-painted finish. This box is prettily decorated with pictures of coloured feathers, cats, flowers and fans, and finished with a pink ribbon border – every girl's treasure box.

MATERIALS

Blank hexagonal cardboard box with lid
Acrylic or household emulsion (latex) paint
Paintbrush
Tea-dyed manuscript paper (see Techniques)
Glue stick
Printed scraps for decoupage: cats, fans, feathers and flowers
Acrylic matt varnish
Tape measure
Scissors
Fabric ribbon
Fabric glue
Assorted buttons
Needle and thread

1 Paint the box inside and out. Here, eau de nil green paint was used. Tear the tea-dyed paper into scraps and glue these to the outer box sides and lid. Stick down the scraps, overlapping them as desired. Varnish the box with two or three coats, allowing each to dry before applying the next.

— TIP —

Before sticking down the ribbon around the box lid, allow the glue to dry slightly as this helps to avoid glue seeping through the fabric.

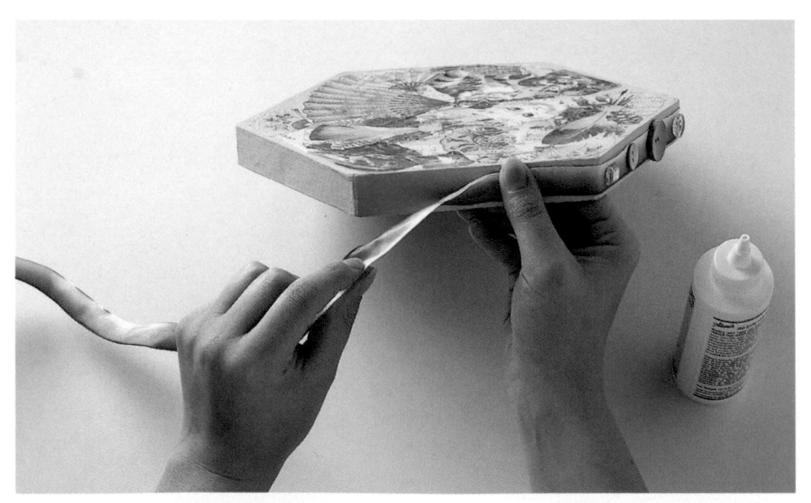

2 Measure the circumference of the rim of the lid. Cut a length of fabric ribbon equal to this measurement. Using fabric glue, stick the ribbon around the rim of the lid. Using the same glue, stick a selection of buttons around the rim on top of the ribbon.

3 Make a simple rosette shape with another length of ribbon. Stitch the central folds down with a needle and thread to secure the shape. Stitch a button on to the centre of the rosette using a needle and thread, then stick the rosette down on to the centre of the box lid to complete the box.

Flowery Faces Album Pages

Here's a project to brighten up those dark winter evenings. Decorate your photo album pages with squares of coloured paper, cut-out summer flowers and jolly family faces. Quick and easy to do, this project will bring a smile to everyone's face.

MATERIALS

Selection of flower pictures
Fine-pointed scissors
Sheets of brightly coloured plain paper
Scissors
Black spiral-bound photo album
Spray adhesive
Children's photographs
Transparent photo corners (optional)

1 Collect flower pictures from magazines, packaging and circulars. Have them colour-photocopied if you need more than you have; change the scale by enlarging and reducing them to achieve a good variety of sizes. Cut out the flowers individually with fine-pointed scissors.

2 Cut out rectangles and squares of coloured plain paper. Arrange them on the black album page and stick them in position with spray adhesive. Arrange the photographs on the background. Either stick them down permanently with adhesive or use transparent photo corners.

3 Arrange the flower cut-outs around the photographs. To avoid sticking them on the actual photographs, arrange them carefully to frame the pictures in a pleasing way. Glue the flowers in place and allow to dry.

Our House

This fold-out display is an ideal showcase for house renovation photographs. Remember to preserve some of that ghastly wallpaper which took you hours of work to remove.

MATERIALS

Three sheets of good quality white or watercolour paper, two to measure 38 x 60cm (15 x 24in) and one 19 x 30cm (7½ x 12in)
Bone folder
Pencil
Metal ruler
Craft knife
Cutting mat
Glue stick
Bulldog clips

1 To make the concertina house on the right of the design, fold the sheet of paper 19 x 30cm (7½ x 12in) in half lengthways, then fold the long ends back to align with the centre fold. Crease the folds using a bone folder. Open the paper out, then fold it in half widthways. Crease the folds. Open out the sheet and mark in the pointed roof sections. Cut out the roof sections. Cut out two small windows from the central sections of the folded paper. Fold the design widthways and glue the outside edges together.

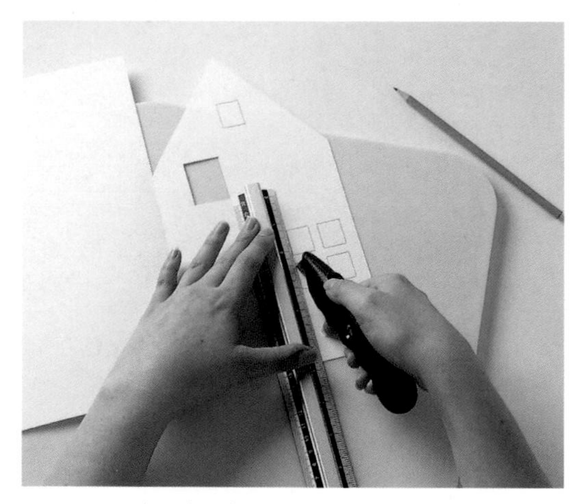

2 To make the folded house at the left of the design, take a large sheet of paper and fold over a third of the paper at the right-hand side. On this third, lightly draw a pointed roof at the top and mark the windows. Cut out the windows as before.

3 For the background, fold over a 2cm (¾in) at the left-hand side of the remaining sheet of white paper. Crease the fold using the bone folder. Glue the larger cut-out house to this flap so that the house can be lifted and turned like the page of a book.

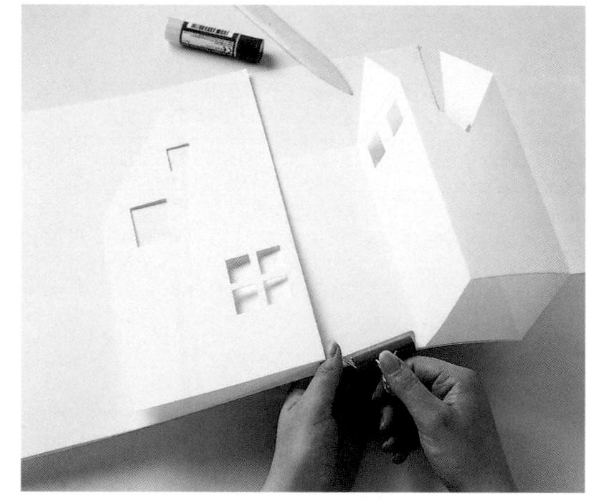

4 Glue the left-hand side of the origami house to the right-hand side of the main album page. Secure the paper with bulldog clips while the glue dries. Arrange photographs and memorabilia in the album pages.

— TIP —

Make the project using scrap paper first to make sure you understand the folding instructions.

Picnic in the Park

This fun collage combines snapshots of an al fresco picnic with cut-outs of cutlery, wine bottles, plates and a picnic basket to tell the story of a happy outing. This is a really enjoyable and simple way to record a memorable day; you could create a collage of a trip to the zoo or a child's birthday party in the same style.

MATERIALS

Magazine pictures of picnic baskets, plates, wine bottles, a rug, cutlery, glasses and food
Scissors
Glue stick
Sheet of green paper
Snapshots of a family picnic
Transparent photo corners

1 Assemble the motifs for the design. Carefully and accurately cut out the pictures of the picnic basket, plates, cutlery, glasses and food using sharp scissors, or a craft knife and working on a cutting mat. Ensure there is no background showing once you have completed the cutting out.

— *TIP* —

Household product catalogues are a good source of material for this project.

2 Glue the sheet of green paper on to the album pages. Stick a picture of a travel rug down in one corner. Arrange photographs of a picnic on the paper, and when you are happy with the design, fix the pictures in place with transparent photo corners.

3 Arrange the other cut-outs decoratively around the collage to fill in the spaces. Some cut-outs can be placed on the rug, and others displayed around the picnic photographs. Glue them all in place.

Patchwork Album Covers

You do not need to be a skilled stitcher to accomplish these album covers. Following the patchwork pattern known as "log cabin", fabric strips are stitched around a central image.

Small Album

MATERIALS

Small album
Tape measure
Dressmaking scissors
Extra heavy non-woven interfacing
Iron-on fusible webbing
Iron
Photo transferred fabric image (see Techniques)
Cotton print fabric in several colours
Sewing machine
Sewing thread

1 Measure the height and width of the opened book; add 2cm (¾in) to the height and 10cm (4in) to the width to allow for hems and side flaps. Following these measurements, cut out a piece of extra heavy non-woven interfacing and a piece of iron-on fusible webbing. Following the manufacturer's instructions, iron the webbing to the interfacing. Peel off the backing paper.

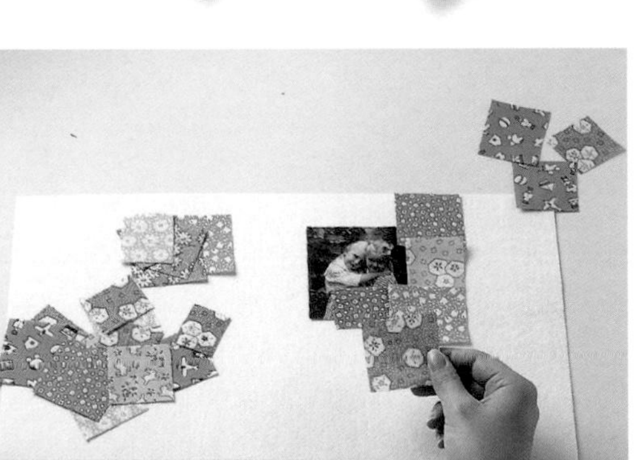

2 Position your chosen photo image on the front cover. Cut scraps of fabric into small squares and rectangles and arrange them around the photo, overlapping them slightly as desired. When you have covered the whole area, cover with a pressing cloth and iron to fuse the scraps to the cover.

3 Topstitch all the raw edges of the patches with a satin stitch. Overcast around the the outer edges of the cover. With right sides together, turn in 5cm (2in) at each short side for the side flaps and pin in place. Stitch a 1cm (½in) seam along each long edge, then turn right side out. Insert the album. ▶

Large Album

MATERIALS

Scrapbook or album
Tape measure
Dressmaking scissors
Cotton print fabrics in several colours
Iron
Sewing machine
Sewing thread
Photo-transferred image (see Techniques)
Pins
Contrasting sewing thread

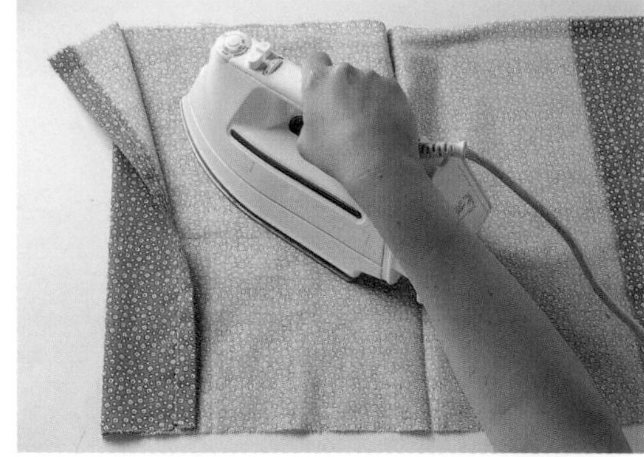

1 Measure the height and width of the book you wish to cover. Add 4cm (1½in) to the height and 20cm (8in) to the width. Cut out a piece of fabric following these measurements. Place the fabric right side down. Fold over a 2cm (¾in) hem at each short side. Press and stitch in place. Fold in another 8cm (3¼in) and press. Fold the fabric in half widthways. Press the centre fold.

2 Turn the fabric right side up. Using the pressed folds as a guide, position the photo image on the front cover and pin the image in place.

3 For the log cabin patchwork design, cut out several strips of fabric each 3cm (1¼in) wide from three or four different colours. Place the first strip right side down on the top edge of the image, lining up the edges. Pin to secure. Cut the strip so it is the same length as the top of the image.

4 Stitch the strip down using a 5mm (¼in) seam allowance. Fold the strip upwards so that the fabric is the right side up and press lightly.

5 Place the second strip right side down on the right-hand side of the first strip and the image, cut away the excess, stitch and fold back. Continue working around the photo in a clockwise direction, stitching down strips of different coloured cotton, until the book front is covered.

6 Turn in the side flaps so that right sides are together and pin. Stitch a 1cm (½in) hem at the top and bottom of the book cover. Clip the corners to neaten them, then turn the fabric flaps right side out. Press the cover. Fold under the raw edge of the log cabin strip on the centre spine, press and stitch down. Trim the strips of the log cabin design along the top, bottom and leading edge, then topstitch all around with a close satin stitch in a contrasting colour to finish the raw edges. Press to neaten. Insert the album.

Album Page for a Baby Boy

Soft pastel shades inspired the look of this album page which has a contemporary style. Keep tiny mementoes, such as the birth tag from the hospital safely inside a small clear plastic envelope.

MATERIALS

Scissors
Pastel-coloured paper
Striped printed paper, such as wallpaper
Heavy white paper
Glue stick
Baby mementoes
Small, clear plastic envelope
White card (card stock)
Pencil
Cork mat or corrugated cardboard
Darning needle
Fancy-edged scissors in two designs
Rotating leather hole punch
Lettering stencil
Craft knife
Cutting mat
Baby ric-rac braid

1 Cut out rectangles of plain and printed paper, and arrange them on the heavy white paper. Use different-sized rectangles to make a pleasing layout. Glue in position. Arrange the collage items on the background. Small mementoes such as identification tags can be placed in small plastic envelopes. Glue the items in place.

2 Take a small piece of white card (card stock) and draw a simple motif, such as a boat, on the wrong side of it. Working on a cork mat or corrugated cardboard to protect the surface, make pinpricks at regular intervals along the outline of the design using a darning needle. Follow the pencil lines as a guide.

3 Cut out a rectangle of blue paper using fancy-edged scissors in a scallop design. Then cut out the pinpricked motif with fancy-edged scissors in a postage stamp design and glue it on to the blue paper.

4 Make a mount for the photograph by cutting out a piece of white card (card stock) larger all round than the photograph, using scallop-edged scissors. Pierce small decorative holes all around the edges of the card using a rotating leather hole punch.

— TIP —

Glue right up to the edges of each item when you are fixing them in position so that they do not lift.

5 Place a lettering stencil over a piece of blue paper and stencil the letter of your choice on the card (card stock). Cut it out carefully with a craft knife, working on a cutting mat.

6 Trim the corners of the letter stencil with scissors to round them gently. Mount the cut-out letter on a rectangle of pale yellow paper, then on to a larger fancy-edged rectangle of white card. Pierce a small hole in the centre top of the card and thread it with baby ric-rac braid. Tie this in a bow. Carefully stick everything down.

Pets' Page

Why not devote one or two pages of your album to your pets? Create a pet montage with cut-out photographs, conventional snapshots and the whole decorated with fun paw prints and cute stickers. Using a combination of rectangular snapshots and cut-outs adds interest to the overall page while the paw prints and stickers add extra colour.

MATERIALS

Photographs of pets
Scissors
Plain paper
Glue stick
Selection of children's stickers of dogs and puppies
Paw print rubber stamp
Several coloured ink pads
Paper towels

1 Decide on the general layout of the album page, then work out which photographs you want to use. Either have some colour-copied, or if you have enough, cut out some of the pets with scissors. Arrange the pictures on the plain paper then, when you are happy with the arrangement, glue the pictures in position. Decorate with stickers and paw prints.

2 For the second pets' page, glue the main photograph on a coloured background, then add stickers all around the photograph to frame it. If you prefer not to stick them directly to the original photograph, have copies made.

3 Complete the design with a paw print rubber stamp. Ink each colour individually, and wash off the colour and pat the stamp dry with a paper towel between applications. Use the stamp either to make a border design or to make random prints at different angles.

Folk Art Album Pages

The colours in the photos of a favourite cat and an equally beloved niece suggested they would work well with the traditional blues, rusts and ochres used in traditional folk art. Both pages use different techniques, but work well together. Some of the printed patterned papers were made by colour photocopying traditional printed cottons used for patchwork.

MATERIALS

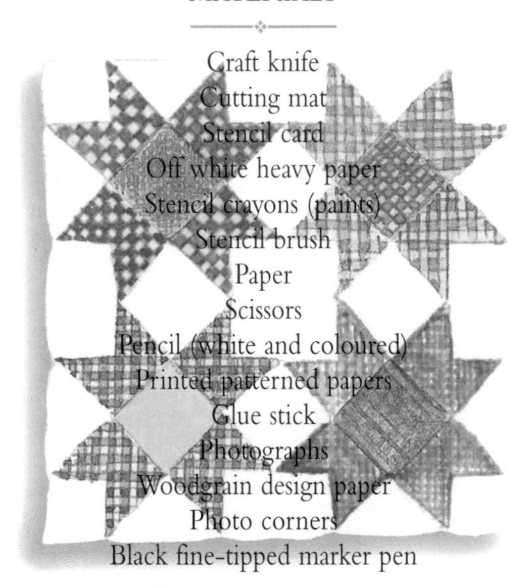

Craft knife
Cutting mat
Stencil card
Off white heavy paper
Stencil crayons (paints)
Stencil brush
Paper
Scissors
Pencil (white and coloured)
Printed patterned papers
Glue stick
Photographs
Woodgrain design paper
Photo corners
Black fine-tipped marker pen

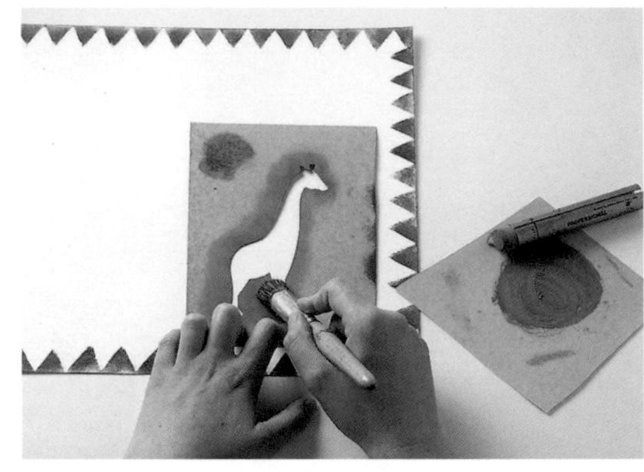

1 Stencil a zigzag border all around a piece of off-white heavy paper using a rust red stencil crayon (paint). Then add Noah's Ark animal stencils (see Templates), leaving room for a photograph. Stencil these images using two-colour stencilling.

2 Make two star templates from paper, one large and one small. Draw around these on printed paper and cut out several of each size. Arrange the stars around the stencilled images and glue them in place. Attach the photograph.

3 For the cat page, assemble a background collage using woodgrain design papers and complementary coloured papers. Cut out triangles of printed paper to stick across each corner. Cut out cat, heart and dove motifs (see Templates) from printed papers.

4 Glue the background papers down on to a foundation sheet of paper the same size as your album pages. Leave a border all around the edges and a strip down one side on which to place the cut-outs. Glue the cut-out motifs in position. Attach the photographs using brown paper gummed photo corners. Finish the page by drawing "stitching" lines around the edges of the collage with a black marker pen.

— TIP —

Stencil crayons are oil-based and should be left to dry out for several days to prevent smudges.

Schooldays

This memento of your schooldays will bring back memories of past escapades, glories and disasters. Indulge yourself and relive them all by making this schoolday album page.

MATERIALS

Sharp scissors
Brick-effect dolls' house paper
Glue stick
Envelope
Selection of school photographs
Transparent photo corners
Small labels
Striped grosgrain ribbon
Metal badge
Cloth badge
School reports
Star stickers

1 Cut out pieces of brick-effect paper to match the album pages and glue in position. Glue the envelope in one corner so that the flap faces upwards. Arrange the photographs on the page then secure with photo corners.

2 Next to each photograph, stick a computer-printed or hand-written label with the year each picture was taken. The album pages here show three generations of school children.

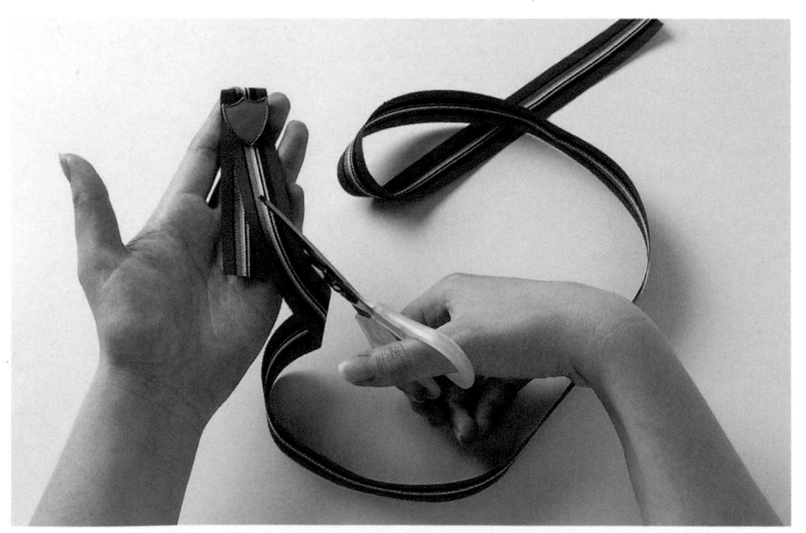

3 Fold the ribbon in half and attach the metal badge to the top of the ribbon. Trim the ribbon ends to create a V shape. (Always keep a sheet of paper between the album pages to prevent the badge damaging the pictures.)

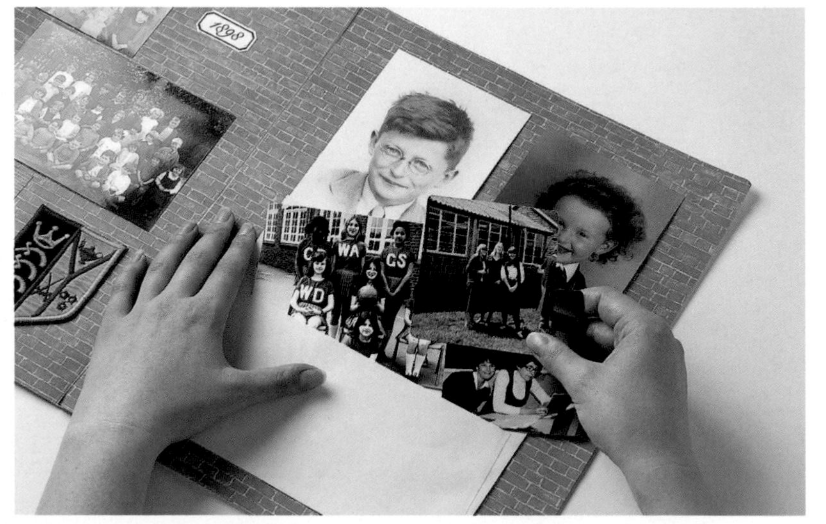

4 Glue a cloth badge to the page, then store extra pictures and school reports in the envelope. Glue the ribbon and badge on top of the flap. Finally, glue a sprinkling of star stickers over the album pages.

1898
1934
1972
1938
1998

Kate
Samuel
Lizzie
Alicia
Hilda
Herbert
Albert
Nellie
Mary
cColin
Jonathan
Michael
Lucinda
Emma

Family Tree

This is a lovely way to record your family tree. Instead of simply drawing a diagram of names and dates, this family tree is decorated with pictures of each family member glued on paper leaves with their details added alongside.

MATERIALS

- Selection of family photos
- Scissors
- Paper
- Pencil
- Two shades of green paper
- Glue stick
- Sheet of marble-effect paper
- Small labels
- Green mount board (optional)

1 Re-photograph the family photographs on a sepia-effect or black and white film, and ensuring that they are all a similar size. Cut out each one carefully.

2 Make a leaf template and draw around it on the wrong side of a piece of green paper. Cut around the outline. Repeat to make a leaf background for each picture, using paper in two shades of green.

3 Glue the photos on to the leaves and allow to dry. Trim away the excess photograph to fit the shape.

4 Arrange the pictures on the marble paper background, with the youngest generation at the bottom, and glue in place. Next to each photograph stick a label in which to add names. If desired, mount the whole family tree on green mountboard to finish.

Wedding Page

This lovely reminder of a special day, featuring the wedding photograph and invitation, and decorated with cut-out doves and hearts, is simple yet effective in black, white and gold. This page can be the first in a wedding album, to be followed by other pictures of the happy day.

MATERIALS

Spiral-bound album
Craft knife
Metal ruler
Cutting mat
Heavy white paper
Fancy-edged scissors
Translucent glassine paper
Glue stick
Wedding photograph
Transparent photo corners
Scissors
Pencil
Gold paper
Gold card (card stock)
Translucent envelope
Wedding mementoes: invitation, pressed flowers, ribbon, confetti

1 Make a protective page for the treasured photograph by cutting a page out of the album to within about 2.5cm (1in) of the spiral binding. Use a craft knife and a metal ruler for a straight edge, and work on a cutting mat to protect the surface.

2 Cut another strip of paper slightly wider than the first strip from another sheet of heavy white paper. Trim one long edge with fancy-edged scissors. Cut a sheet of glassine paper or other translucent paper the same size as the album pages.

— TIP —

If you have colour negatives of an occasion, you can have black and white prints made from them.

3 Glue the glassine paper to the tab in the album, then cover this with the single strip of paper with the decorative edge visible. The translucent protective sheet should now be sandwiched between the two tabs. Allow to dry.

4 Assemble the photograph display. Using fancy-edged scissors, cut around the edges of a piece of heavy white paper slightly larger than the photograph. Mount the photo on this using transparent photo corners.

5 Make several dove and heart motifs templates (see Templates). Trace around them on to the wrong side of gold paper and white heavy paper. Reverse the dove motif so that they face in different directions. Cut each out.

6 To assemble the album page, stick down a piece of gold card slightly larger than the mounted photo. Add a translucent envelope containing a memento of the occasion such as an invitation, together with any other small saved pressed flowers, ribbon, confetti or similar. Place some of the motifs you have cut out inside the envelope too. Glue down the mounted photograph. Stick the dove and heart cut-outs on to the page in a pleasing arrangement.

Memory Quilt

This beautiful album quilt was made to commemorate the 70th birthday of the maker's mother. Some of the ivory silk fabric used was from a wedding dress with particular sentimental value.

MATERIALS

Black and white photographs
Scraps of ivory silk in a variety of textures and shades
Transfer paper
Iron
Paper
Pencil
Dressmaking scissors
Calico
Tape measure
Pins
Sewing machine
Ivory cotton sewing thread
Ivory silk for the quilt backing
Quilt interlining
Coffee silk for binding the edges
Metallic sewing thread

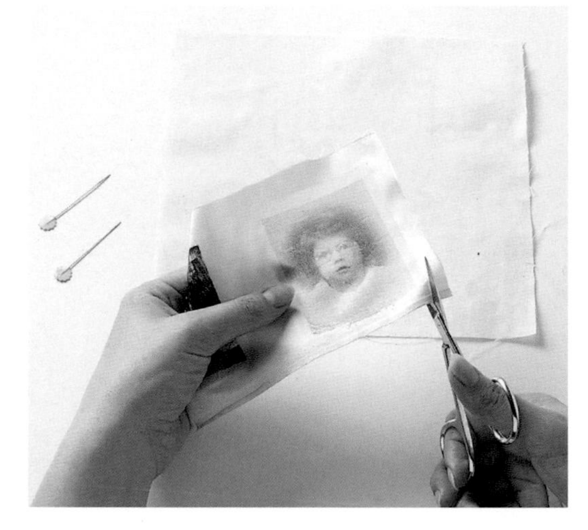

1 Transfer the photographs on to silk. Use a transfer paper that does not require excessive or prolonged heat to be effective, as silk is more prone to scorching than cotton. Decide on the finished block size and estimate how many blocks you will need to make by working out a simple plan on paper. Cut the block squares from plain calico, adding a seam allowance all around of 2cm (¾in). Trim each transferred photograph and pin to the block through the border of the photograph to avoid damaging the print. Repeat for each block.

2 Cut random strips of various weights and textures of silks. Pin one strip right side down on one side of the photograph at an angle. Using a sewing machine, sew the first strip down, then flip over to conceal the stitching and press lightly.

3 Add further strips at an angle working in a clockwise direction, covering the end of the previous strip as you proceed. Cut away excess fabric from each strip before stitching the next.

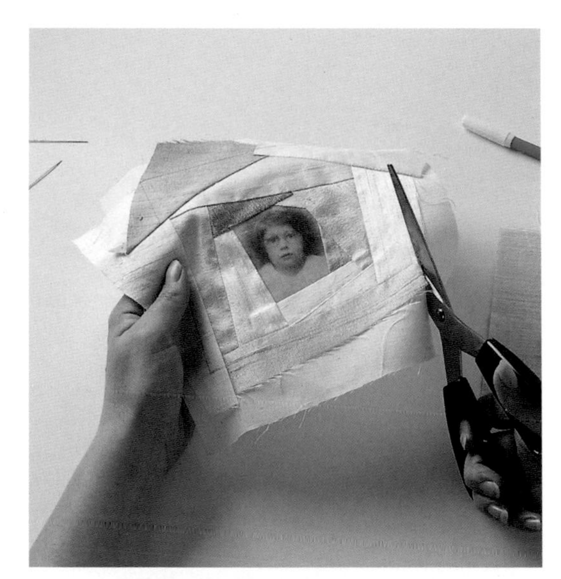

4 Repeat for each calico block. When you have added all the strips, press the patch then trim away the excess with scissors, leaving a 2cm (¾in) seam allowance.

5 Pin and stitch the blocks together, adding extra strips between the blocks (sashing strips). Join the blocks in rows according to your plan then add a border around the edge. To assemble the quilt, place the backing right side down on a clean, flat surface, then place the interlining on top. Finally place the quilt top right side up on top. Baste all three layers together.

6 Decorate the quilt with machine or hand quilting before binding the edges with silk. Finish the design with machine embroidery using metallic thread in a zigzag or other embroidery stitch.

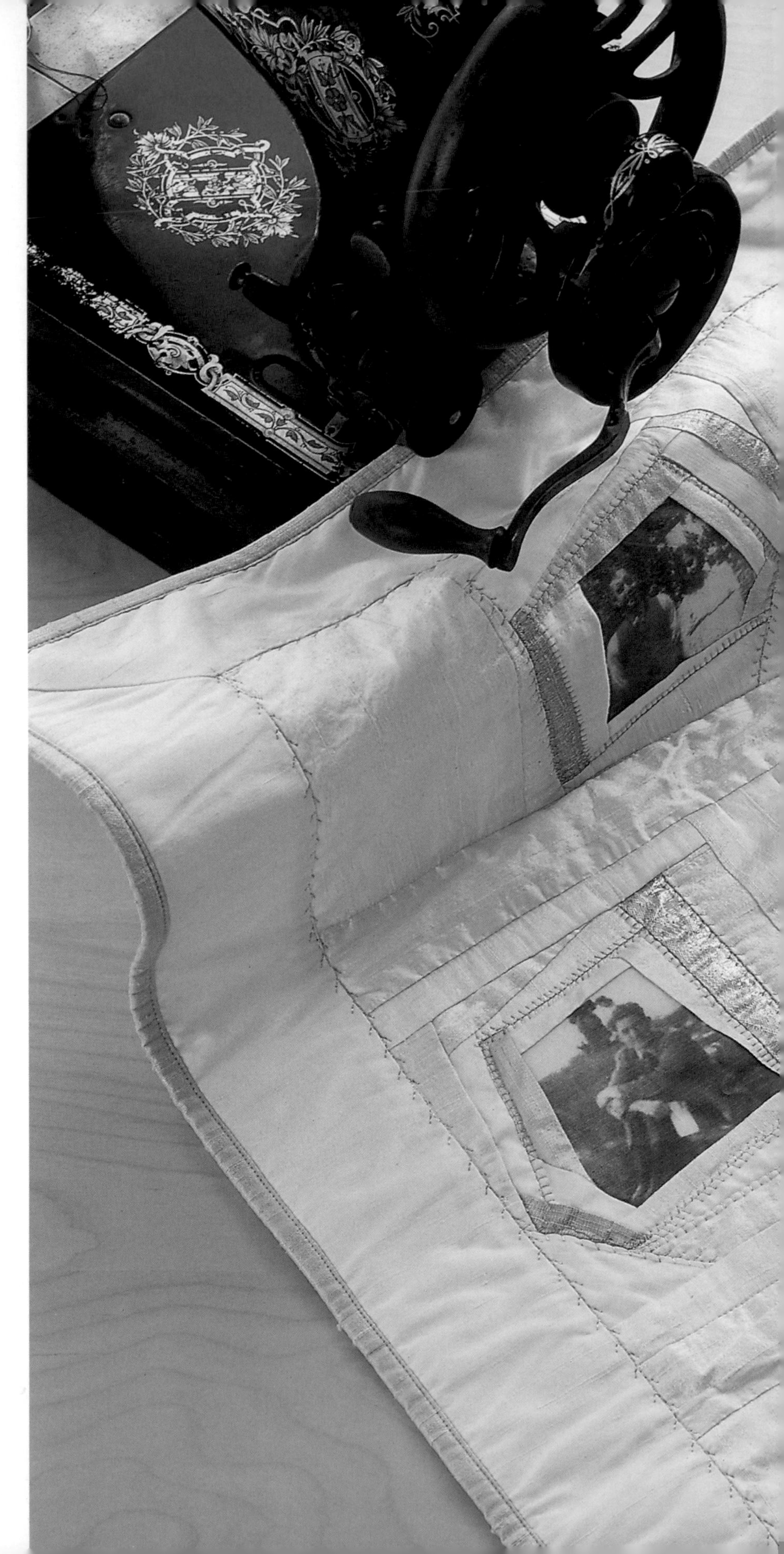

Christmas Scraps Page

Commemorate a special Christmas by making a festive page for your album. Traditional yuletide printed scraps are readily available from craft shops, or save the decorations from Christmas crackers and packaging and use these to decorate the page.

MATERIALS

Small scissors
Printed Victorian Christmas scraps used for decoupage
Glue stick
Gold embossed paper ribbon trim or other decoupage border
Sheet of red card (card stock)
Bone folder
Christmas photographs
Transparent photo corners

1 Carefully cut out Christmas motifs from decorative Victorian scraps using small scissors. Stick lengths of gold paper ribbon trim or other decoupage border at angles across the corners of a sheet of red card (card stock). This will be the background of the page.

2 Arrange the Christmas motifs on the album page so that they form a frame around the centre. When you are happy with their position, glue them down to secure each in place. Place a piece of scrap paper over the motifs and smooth them down with a bone folder. Attach your Christmas photographs in the centre of the page using transparent photo corners.

— TIP —

As an alternative to decoupage scraps, try using Christmas stamps such as holly leaves inked with gold. Choose a lighter tone of background paper if you choose to use stamps.

Contemporary Collection

This fascinating collection of ephemera gives a snapshot of life today. You can include stamps, money, tickets, product labels, snippets of handwriting, tiny cut-out sections from a newspaper, photos, pressed flowers, snippets of fabric, sweet papers and anything else you want. Make the collection as general or as personal as you like.

MATERIALS

Craft knife
Metal ruler
Cutting mat
Translucent polythene board
Transparent file pockets for 3.5cm (1½in) film or stamp collecting
Collection of ephemera: stamps, foreign money, tickets, labels, etc
Clear plastic laminating film
Hole punch
Handmade paper
Hinged metal rings

1 Using a craft knife and metal ruler and working on a cutting mat, cut two pieces of polythene board slightly larger than the clear file pockets you intend to use. Decorate the cover with a small collage of flat ephemera. Cover with laminating film for protection. Repeat on the inside of the cover, working over the same area as you did on the front to mask the reverse of the first collage. Cover with another piece of laminating film.

2 Make holes in the front and back cover with a single hole punch to correspond with the clear plastic file pockets.

3 Fill the plastic pockets with your collection of ephemera. Items can include foreign money, stamps, feathers, or even packaging. Make a pleasing arrangement as you work.

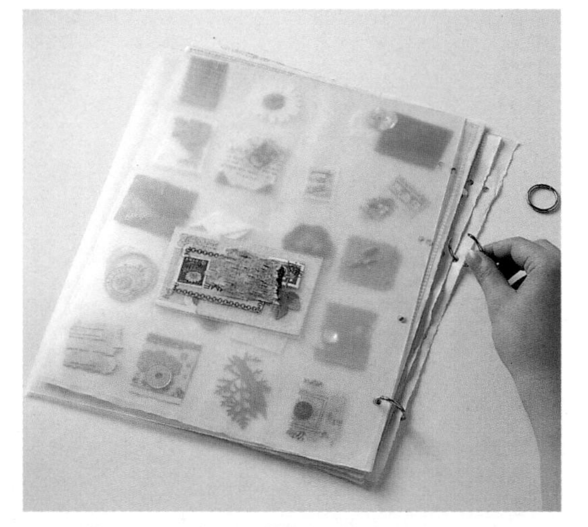

4 When you have filled all the pockets, make holes in the handmade paper to correspond with the file pockets. Interleave these with the plastic file pockets. Assemble the album by stacking the file pockets and paper in between the front and back covers. Join together with hinged metal rings.

J.&P.COATS
TRADE MARK
MAGYAR POSTA

Family in the Garden

Summer days are often spent in the garden, having lunch or a drink and chatting with family and friends. Keep a record of this part of life by making a garden collage using photos, stamped garden designs and pressed flowers and leaves.

MATERIALS

Selection of rubber stamps with a garden theme: plant pots, flowers, garden tools
Selection of papers in shades of green, brown and off-white
Ink pads in black and dark green
Paper towels
Fancy-edged paper scissors
Scissors
Family photos in the garden
Sheet of brown paper
Gummed brown paper photo corners
Glue stick
Selection of pressed flowers and leaves

1 Stamp several versions of garden-theme designs on a selection of coloured and textured paper using black and dark green ink. Clean the stamps between different colours with paper towels. Allow to dry.

2 Cut out some of the stamped motifs with fancy-edged scissors and others with ordinary scissors. Tear around the edges of other motifs to create a rough edge.

3 Arrange the photos on the foundation page. When you are happy with the arrangement, stick the pictures down with gummed brown paper photo corners.

4 Assemble the collage by adding the different stamped motifs, pressed flowers and leaves. Glue each item in position.

Fabric-covered Memory Box

Everyone needs a special box in which to put their favourite things. This lilac linen box tied with ribbons is especially pretty and ideal for storing letters, photographs and treasures. This box would make a lovely gift for a daughter, niece or granddaughter.

MATERIALS

Cutting mat
Craft knife
Metal ruler
Strong cardboard
Paper
Pencil
Scissors
Pins
Pale lilac linen
Dressmaking scissors
Basting thread
Needle
Narrow velvet ribbon
Grosgrain ribbon
Ric-rac braid
Sewing machine
Sewing thread
Iron
Small embroidered motif
Fabric glue

1 Working on a cutting mat and using a craft knife and metal ruler, from strong cardboard cut out a base and a lid, each 19.4 x 15.4cm (7½ x 6in); two long sides each 19.4 x 7.4cm (7½ x 3in); and two short sides each 15.4 x 7.4cm (6 x 3in). These will be used to slip inside the fabric cover to make the box rigid.

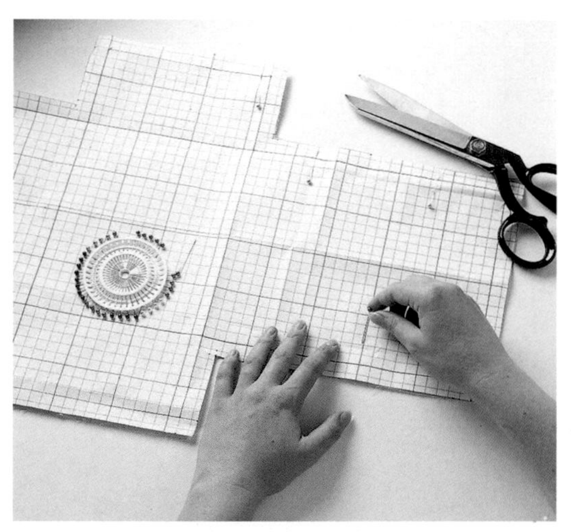

2 Make a paper pattern using the measurements on the template as a guide. Add a 1.5cm (½in) seam allowance all around the pattern. Pin the pattern to a piece of lilac linen folded in half and cut out two pieces of fabric.

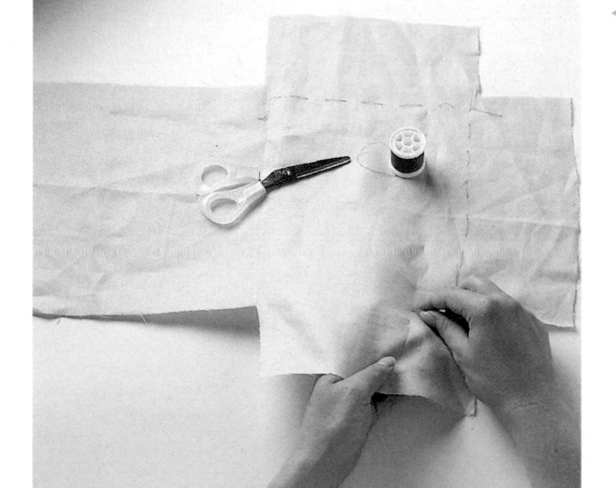

3 Using a contrasting coloured thread, and working on the piece of fabric intended for the right side, baste the fabric to mark out the stitching lines for the different sections of the box.

4 Cut eight lengths of velvet ribbon for the corner ties and two lengths of grosgrain ribbon for the front ties. On the right side of the fabric (the large square) pin and baste a length of ric-rac braid to the line marked in contrasting thread along three sides of the box lid. Pin the ribbon ties in place and pin one piece of the grosgrain ribbon to the lid.

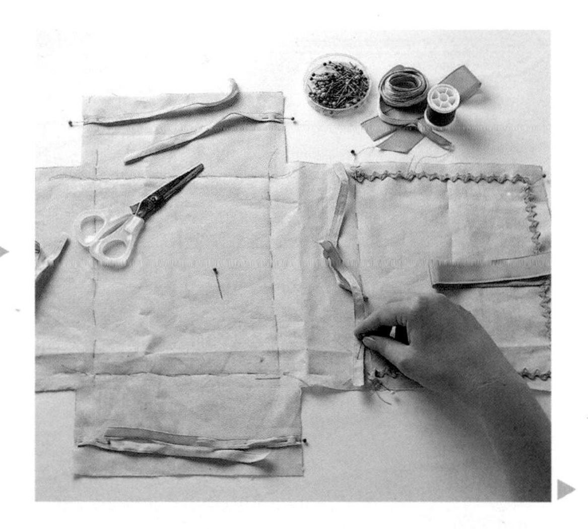

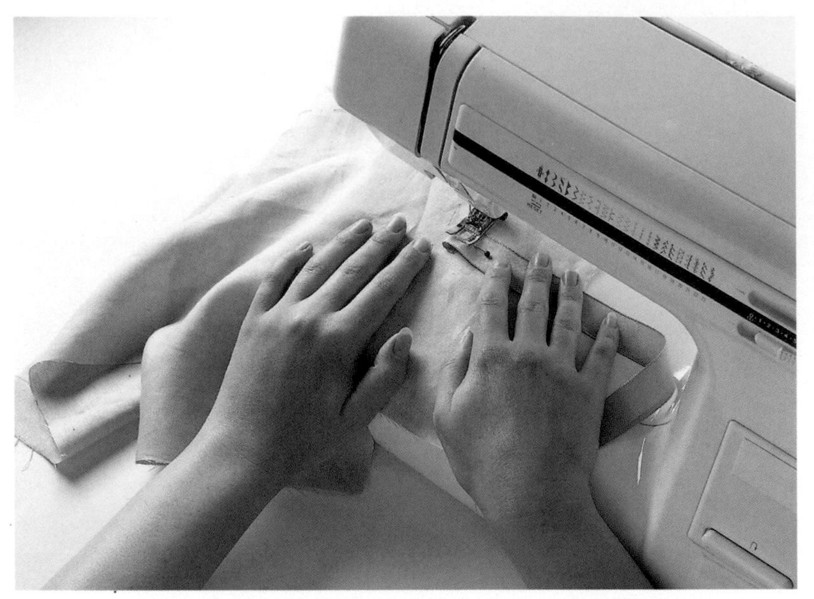

5 Pin the last piece of grosgrain ribbon to the centre of the long front section, but on the wrong side of the fabric. Stitch the ribbon ties down with a straight machine stitch, turning the raw edges underneath to neaten.

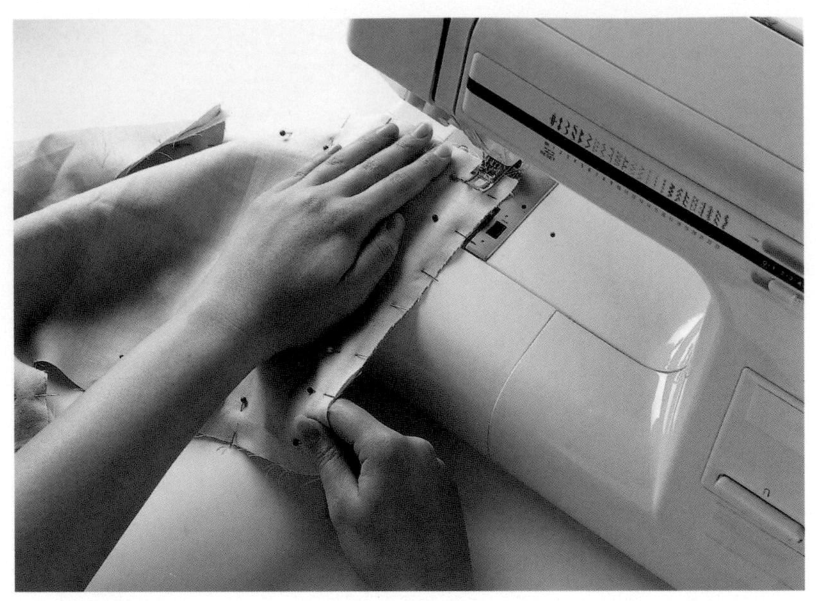

6 Pin the two pieces of fabric right sides together, then taking a 1.5cm (½in) seam allowance, stitch all around the edges of the box. Leave the long side of the 19.4 x 15.4cm (7½ x 6in) rectangle open so that the cardboard can be slipped inside. Clip the corners and trim the seam allowance, then turn the box through to the right side and press.

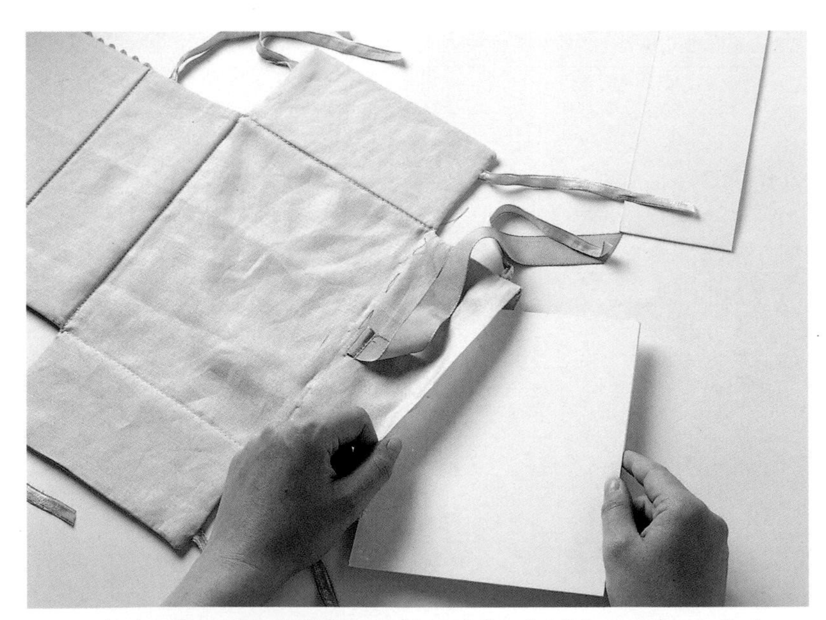

7 Push the first piece of the cardboard for the lid area through the opening along the long side. Neatly stitch along the lid edge to enclose it using a zipper foot on the machine. Insert the cardboard for the long side and enclose with a line of stitches, followed by the pieces for the short sides, the large piece for the base and the final piece for the last long side. Enclose the card with a line of stitches.

8 When all the cardboard is stitched in place, neatly slipstitch the opening closed. Glue an embroidered motif on to the box lid with fabric glue. Then tie the ribbon ties at each corner to assemble the box.

Butterfly Bonanza

If you like butterflies then you'll love this project. Coloured paper butterflies flutter prettily around a lovely card and photo mailer, seeming to fly out of the paper itself. Work slowly and carefully to cut out the intricate filigree decoration on the butterflies' wings.

MATERIALS

- Pencil
- Paper
- Scissors
- Selection of pastel-coloured papers, including white
- Cutting mat
- Craft knife
- Revolving leather punch
- Fancy-edged scissors
- Fine corrugated white cardboard
- Glue stick
- Heavy white paper
- Photographs
- Transparent photo corners

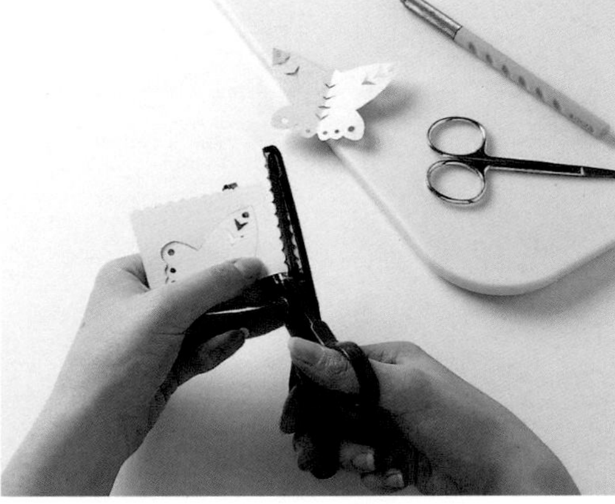

1 Enlarge the butterfly motif (see Templates) in three different sizes and cut them out. Place a template on folded paper and trace around it. Cut out the shapes in the wings with a craft knife and make decorative holes with a leather punch. Cut out the butterfly with scissors. Make a selection of butterfly motifs in different sizes and colours.

2 To make the half butterfly card, trace the butterfly on to a piece of coloured paper, placing the fold line of the butterfly slightly away from the edge of the paper. Make the holes and decorative cuts as before, then cut around the butterfly wings with a craft knife, avoiding cutting along the fold line.

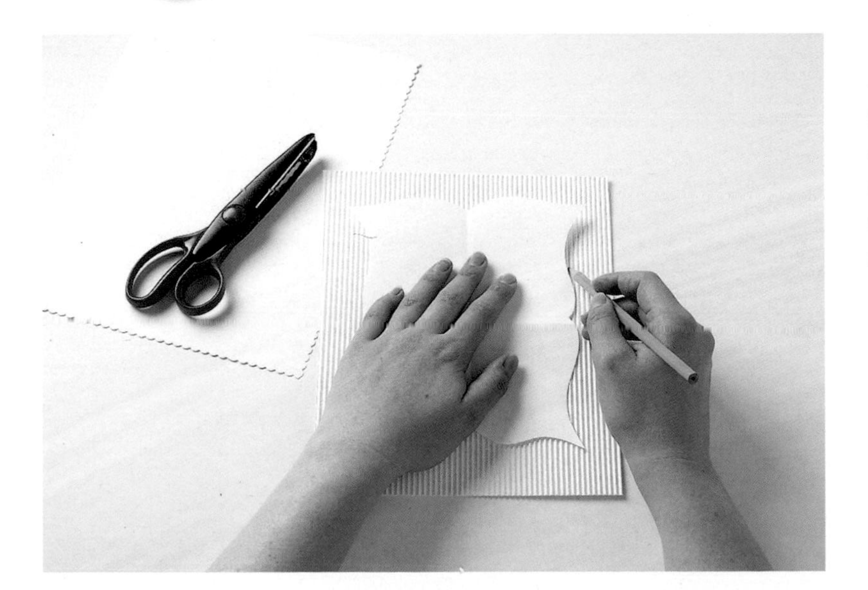

3 Fold the motif outwards to make a crease along the centre line. Cut around the edges with fancy-edged scissors. Make a foundation on which to mount the butterflies using corrugated cardboard. Enlarge the frame template to size then cut it out carefully from the corrugated card, taking care not to crush the ridges. Glue the cut-out on to a slightly larger rectangle of heavy white paper and mount it on a larger piece of coloured paper, if desired.

4 Carefully make a tiny mark where you intend to mount the photograph, then arrange the butterfly motifs around the frame, slotting some individual butterflies inside the winged cards. Finally, attach the photograph to the picture using transparent photo corners.

5 Make the photo mailer from a long strip of heavy white paper, cut slightly wider than the photo and long enough to enclose the picture with a flap for the butterfly. Cut out one small and one large butterfly motif from coloured paper, then cut out a half motif from one end of the photo mailer.

6 Assemble the photo mailer by sticking the large single butterfly to the front of the card in such a position that the wings slot through the folded half motif cut in the mailer itself. The action of slotting the wings together will keep the card closed. Stick a small motif on the front of the card and mount the photograph inside with transparent photo corners.

— TIP —

Adapt the photo mailer for a birth announcement. Have colour copies made of your baby's photograph or make a print from a tiny foot and photocopy it.

Templates

Enlarge the templates to the desired size on a photocopier.

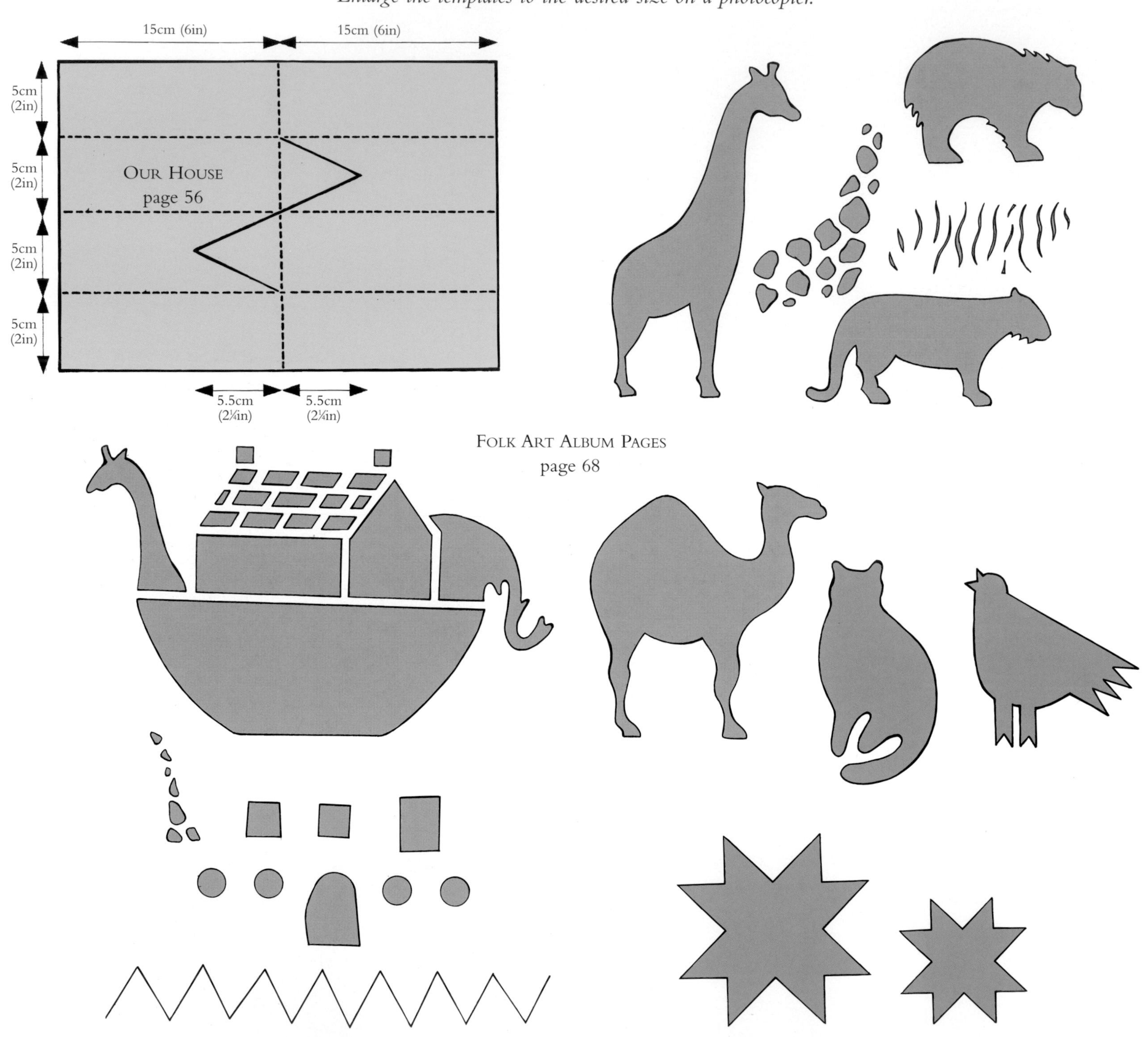

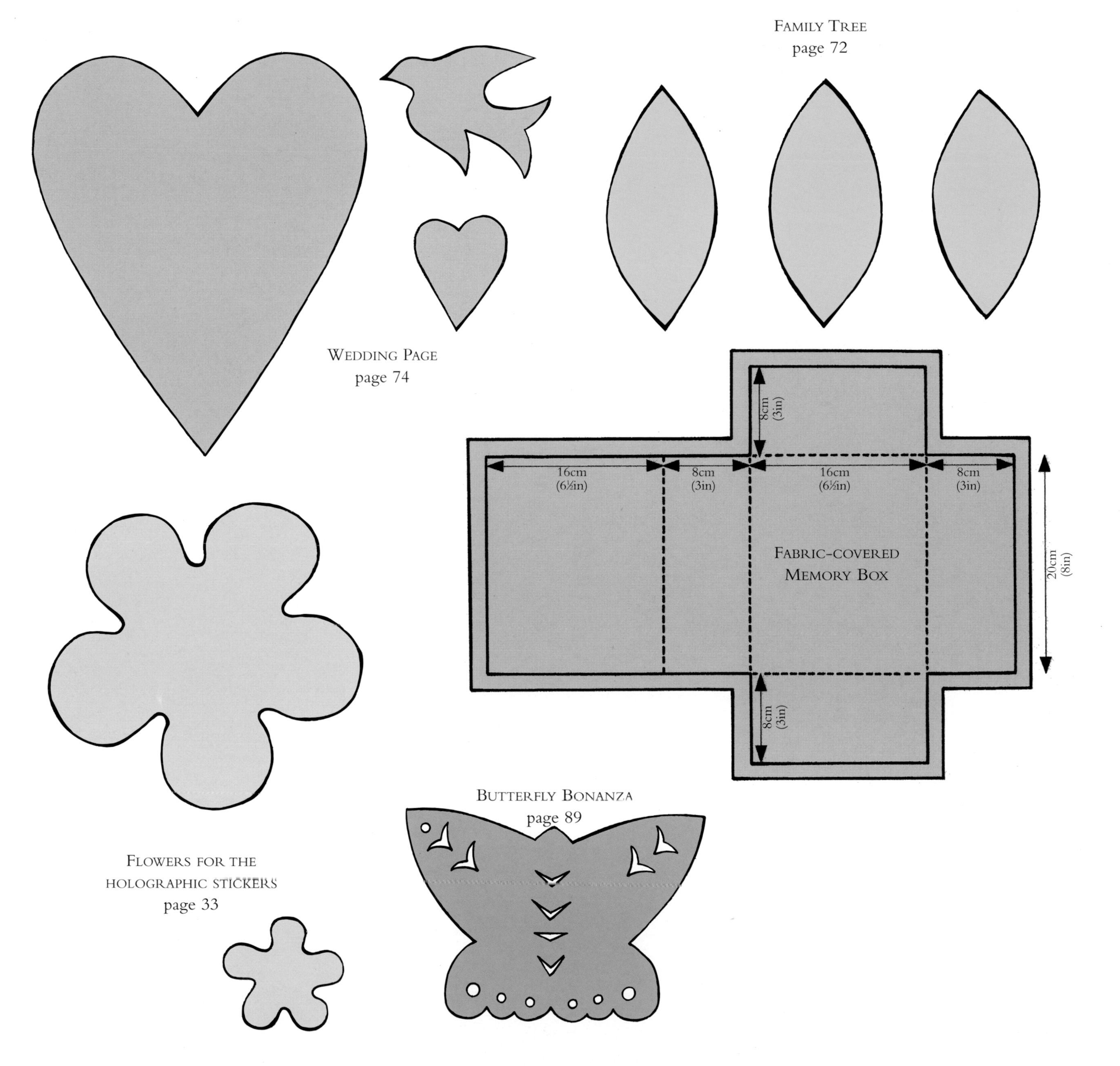
FAMILY TREE
page 72
WEDDING PAGE
page 74
16cm
(6½in)
8cm
(3in)
16cm
(6½in)
8cm
(3in)
8cm
(3in)
8cm
(3in)
20cm
(8in)
FABRIC-COVERED
MEMORY BOX
FLOWERS FOR THE
HOLOGRAPHIC STICKERS
page 33
BUTTERFLY BONANZA
page 89

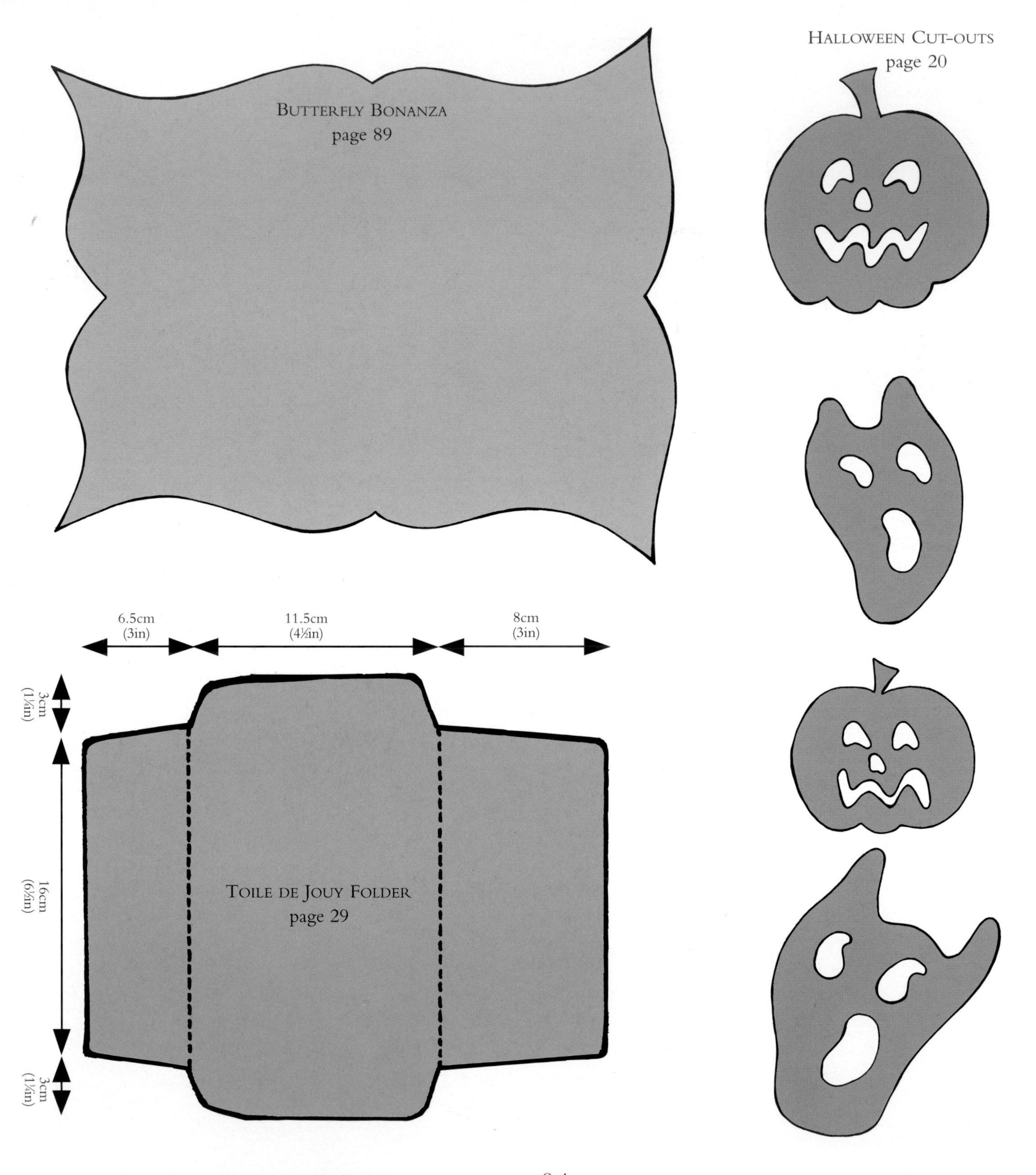
Halloween Cut-outs
page 20
Butterfly Bonanza
page 89
6.5cm
(3in)
11.5cm
(4½in)
8cm
(3in)
3cm
(1¼in)
16cm
(6¼in)
3cm
(1¼in)
Toile de Jouy Folder
page 29

Suppliers

US
Twinrocker Handmade Paper
100 East Third Street
P.O. Box 413
Brookston
Indiana 47923
Tel: (765) 563 3119
Fax: (765) 563 8946
www.twinrocker.com

Dick Blick Art Materials
P.O. Box 1267
695 US Highway 150 East
Galesburg, IL 61402
www.dickblick.com

Craft King
P.O. Box 90637
Lakeland, FL 33804
Tel: (800) 769-9494
www.craft-king.com

The Jerry's Catalog
P.O. Box 58638
Raleigh, NC 27658
Tel: (800) U-ARTIST
www.jerryscatalog.com

Art Supply Warehouse
5325 Departure Drive
North Raleigh, NC 27616
Tel: (919) 878-5077
www.aswexpress.com

Craft Catalog
P.O. Box 1069
Reynoldsburg, OH 43068
Tel: (800) 777-1442

UK
Falkiner Fine Papers
76 Southampton Row
London WC1
Tel: 020 7831 1151

Fred Aldous
PO Box 135
37 Lever Street
Manchester
M1 1LW
Tel: 0161 236 2477

VV Rouleaux
Sloane Square
London W1
Tel: 020 7730 3125

Paperchase
Tottenham Court Road
London
Tel: 020 7323 3707

AUSTRALIA
A to Z Art Supplies
50 Brunswick Terrace
Wynn Vale, SA
Tel: (08) 8289 1202

Art & Craft Warehouse
19 Main Street
Pialba, QLD 4655
Tel: (07) 4124 2581

ACKNOWLEDGEMENTS
The author and publisher would like to thank the following for their contributions:
Sue Hallifax for the Memory Quilt and the Patchwork Album Covers
Lucinda Ganderton for the Schooldays, Picnic, Family Tree and Album for a Baby Girl
Gloria Nicol for the Fabric-covered Memory Box
Mary Maguire for the Egg and Feather Artist's Portfolio, Scottie Dog Album, Log Book and Shell Album

Index

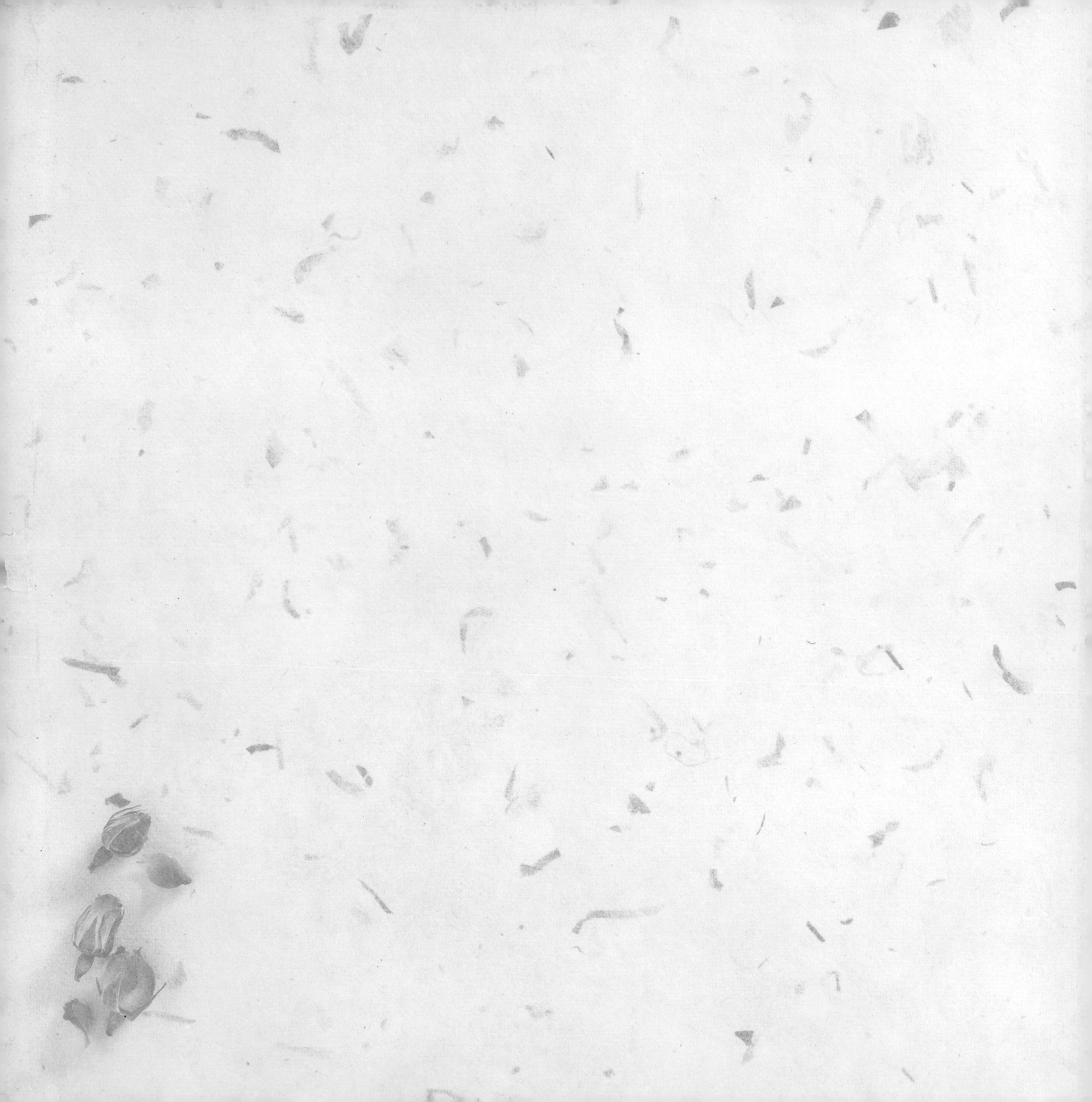